BOOKS BY

REYNOLDS PRICE

THE USE OF FIRE 1990

NEW MUSIC 1990

THE TONGUES OF ANGELS 1990

CLEAR PICTURES 1989

GOOD HEARTS 1988

A COMMON ROOM 1987

THE LAWS OF ICE 1986

KATE VAIDEN 1986

PRIVATE CONTENTMENT 1984

MUSTIAN 1983

VITAL PROVISIONS 1982

THE SOURCE OF LIGHT 1981

A PALPABLE GOD 1978

EARLY DARK 1977

THE SURFACE OF EARTH 1975

THINGS THEMSELVES 1972

PERMANENT ERRORS 1970

LOVE AND WORK 1968

A GENEROUS MAN 1966

THE NAMES AND FACES OF HEROES 1963

A LONG AND HAPPY LIFE 1962

THE USE OF FIRE

REYNOLDS PRICE

THE USE OF FIRE

ATHENEUM

NEW YORK   1990

COLLIER MACMILLAN CANADA
TORONTO

MAXWELL MACMILLAN INTERNATIONAL
NEW YORK   OXFORD   SINGAPORE   SYDNEY

Some of these poems have appeared in earlier forms: THE AMERICAN VOICE
At Sea, Paid; Sky, Dark. AMPERSAND Noon Rest, Best Day. THE ARCHIVE
Again, Half of Life, Initiation, Praise, Valentine. Heron. ATLANTA Farewell
with Photographs. BLACK WARRIOR REVIEW First Love. CARÇANET Winter.
THE CHATTAHOOCHIE REVIEW Easter Sunday 1989. FOR ROBERT PENN WARREN
Socrates and Alcibiades. THE KENTUCKY REVIEW Samuel Barber, Stephen
Spender. LESSON LEARNED Monday, June the Sixth. THE NEW VIRGINIA
REVIEW An Iron Bed in Granville County. THE NEW YORKER Spring Takes the
Homeplace. THE ONTARIO REVIEW Three Dead Voices. THE PARIS REVIEW
A Single Bed, A Back Street in Venice. POETRY An Afterlife, Back, Easter
Sunday 1986, Good Friday; A Heron, A Deer—A Single Day; Juncture,
Near a Milestone, The Resident Heron, Unbeaten Play. PRAIRIE SCHOONER
Antipodes, 1 January 1990, Spirit Flesh. CROSS CURRENTS Two Caves, A House,
A Garden, A Tomb. THE SEWANEE REVIEW First Green, Jim Dead of AIDS,
Lights Out. THE SOUTHERN HUMANITIES REVIEW 13 February 1984–90.
THE SOUTHERN REVIEW 15 March 1987, Giant, The Rack, 16 March 1987.
THE SOUTHWEST REVIEW Safekeeping. TRIQUARTERLY The Eel.

Copyright © 1990 by Reynolds Price

Atheneum
Macmillan Publishing Company
866 Third Avenue, New York, NY 10022

Collier Macmillan Canada, Inc.
1200 Eglinton Avenue East, Suite 200
Don Mills, Ontario M3C 3N1

Library of Congress Cataloging-in-Publication Data
Price, Reynolds, 1933–
    The use of fire / Reynolds Price.
       p.   cm.
    ISBN 0–689–12109–1
    I. Title.
PS3566.R54U8   1990
811'.54—dc20   90–675   CIP

10   9   8   7   6   5   4   3   2   1

Printed in the United States of America

CONTENTS

ONE

TWO: DAYS AND NIGHTS 2

THREE

ONE

UNBEATEN PLAY

FOR ROSS QUAINTANCE (1957–1985)

The night before you die, you wake at four—
Dredged by fear from sleep and forced to thread
A tunnel narrower than Mother's pelvis
(The straits you breeched to win your short good life).
   Arms and legs pinned helpless to your sides,
Your putty skull compressed by bony walls—
Red glow, furred bats, avid scorpions
Line the bore and prise your parching lips.
You warn yourself you've got long years for this
Nocturnal useless hateful self-corrosion,
Visions of a likely private future.
   Twenty fierce uninterrupted minutes
And then you halt. Same appalling goal
You reach each time you slide the airless mine—
The fate that pulverized your neck last week
Returning from a camping trip in Canada,
Crossing a murderous drunk in a hurtling truck:
You're quadriplegic now and twenty-seven.
   You lie balked in hushed officious dark,
No human face at hand but desert time
And tenor mumbles from the neighbor bed,
"Jesus Christ, I'm hurting bad as You."
   Guessing the pain of three hours' crucifixion—
Spiked through the flesh to crossed rough-hewn beams,
Mother and toothless female friends for witness
While cell by cell the rusty blood swags down
A flogged and foul disjointed naked body
In April sun toward winter-famished dirt—
You lay the guess beside your situation,
Know you understand Christ's final scream,
Corroborate the neighbor's grisly claim.
   So in your mind judicious howls bloom,
Each silent as the pulped nerves in your spine.

You let them swarm the ceiling, walls, stone floor.
Then, drained for now, you nap—a jittery mercy.

Here and nowhere else, my care might serve.
If I knew of your wreck, your whereabouts,
I could attempt to press a gentle dream—
Short but true shared ancient memory—
Against the thousand miles and touch your mind
Till intervening sleep might cool the hours
That throng from here till death pervades the room.
  You're three years old, summer of 1960,
Coastal South Carolina, Pawleys Island.
You, your parents, Kathryn your one sister,
Andrew (a friend) and I have come to buy
A slow week here surrendered to the sun,
Broiled seafood, surf—its ceaseless light-and-dark
Combine of chores: washing, soothing, dissolution,
Death (the night we check in, one creased local codger
Tells of a neat tall German washed up here
In 1942 from a depth-charged sub
With, in his pocket, one soaked canceled ticket
From two nights earlier—a Charleston movie).
  I swim with you, your guard, each sunstruck day
Knowing I couldn't save you from this friend,
This mother-warm embracing buoyant sea
Ready to be the sudden father-throat
Grinding you to death, its other chore.
I even warn you, young as you are now,
Not to trust me—guard yourself, guard me.
  So that day on, you laugh and cluck your warning,
"Reynolds, watch your knees! They're getting wet!"
Or "Reynolds, help, my ears are sinking fast!"
  And our minds loosen, mine at least, lean back
Through that whole blessed arc of restful days;
Smile at a sky unblemished far as Asia
And slowly learn to trust each other's claims
(That we're sufficient guards—me, you; you me)

When all we ever manage to become
Is loving, happy, lying in our teeth.

That's my memory anyhow, pressed toward you—
That and my own deck of images
Which might be added to the wishful dream:
    The night I watch your willing harassed father
Herd you toward bed, "Ross, it's time to pee."
You hold out, pounding through the hot apartment
Naked as any newt in spastic glee
Till he exasperates "If you don't hurry,
I'll flush myself down this john and drown."
You still refuse. He flushes, gurgles loudly.
You hurry to the toilet, search the bowl—
Your grinning father in plain sight beside us—
Then look to me and grimly nod "He did it!"

Even in babyhood you generated,
Instead of other babies' farce and yells,
A mainly steady field of dignity.
A strong boy basted brown, your golden hair
Towed by a sun that tormented my hide,
The legs that later thrust you through all sports
Already firming in the slumbrous thighs—
You handed us each day your demonstration:
    Children grand as you are oracles,
Speaking (before they speak) of their grand sender
And His specific will to bless our eyes—
Maker, molder, keeper, sun of all,
Lord of surf and hemlocks, drunks in trucks,
Lord Who this week clubbed you to the Earth
Efficiently as any tortured madman.

Had I known where you lay, had I succeeded
In my dumb hope to lighten your close dark
And press those childish laughing memories
Against your boiling present—any help?

*

5

Forgive the living their least helpful dream,
Our craving to rig smiles on failing lips
And win a merit for the clownish service—
Another soul winged off, wreathed in grins.
    You in your knowing smile can now afford
To free me from this hook and condescend
Majestic thanks toward my shamed regret.

I never saw you in the pitch of manhood,
Heard of your death from distant friends too late
To tell your family my useless sorrow,
So what's this speech but an earnest tardy try
At my own demonstration?—*You endure.*
    Here in these lines, my mind that generates them,
Your brief life burns, will burn through time
And past the eye of time's own frying end.
The vaster mind that sent these lines sent you,
Sent me to know you at the gleaming start
And cut your image deep in human words—
That mind has you forever safe in hand.

Confide me then one sight however quick
Of that new home and your perpetual work.
Return in this world's voice and let us glimpse
The harbor carved in bliss for you and us.
Your old shed pain is only ours now—
Watching your vacant figure in our rooms,
Concave statues of you in dim corners;
Betting on endless day, your new address

—"*In glory, gorgeous fair unbeaten play*
On emerald lawns (the game of stellar love)
Where I in spotless uniform fire teams
Of souls like mine, last seen in agony."

Thanks from now until our boundless meeting.

SOCRATES AND ALCIBIADES

"Such steady worship, sainted Socrates,
   For one young man? Surely you know better?
    Why these ardent gazes,
     Fit for gods?"

Who thinks deepest loves the liveliest,
   Who looks farthest ascertains the heights—
    Sages often bend
     At last to beauty.

after Hölderlin

THREE DEAD VOICES

1. DIRECTOR

Sudden Night was my last play—one cocky
Boy, one spunky girl spar for two hours;
Then force themselves to bend and bear each other's
Fate till death breaks every human vow.
I was hardly into my fourth decade; so *Death*
And *Vow* were words on stage, not earnest monsters
In my room.
                              I'd spent ten years in eager service—
Charming the calmer upper senses of ticket-
Holders with my invisible puppeteer-hands,
Galvanizing actors' bodies in flattering
Light and, in off-moments, galvanizing
My own frail bones with every jolt of male
Voltage I could scrounge or beg (I never bought).
   The final list of names of every man
I knew went past three hundred—not to speak
Of the humpy mob of nameless faceless flat-
Forgot men hotter than light, one or more
Of whom passed me the death I then passed round
In murderous oblivion.
                              Vows? Two years before
I died, I found one sane magnanimous man.
We vowed—one life from there till night, the final
Dark so far ahead it loomed no bigger
Than a lone starved bat on the evening sky.
   No one did what I did better.
Few were smarter, saw the world clearer,
Laughed any kinder.
                              Stand here please—
No closer, *there*—and hope with me

I have not also blindly killed
The same unfailing man I vowed
To keep and guard.

2. PHOTOGRAPHER

I was the prince of thieves of faces in my
Short time, my wallowing city.

The gold and silver, nickel and lead poets,
Novelists, dramatists, dancers

Came for metamorphosis—I
Only, in my time

And country, wielded the precise arcana,
Spells and charms to lure

Scared souls from their black lairs to harmless day—
Outrageous blooms of the covert

Self: this grove of orchids I abandoned,
Grown from simple light.

By night I lurked stock-still, disguised as one
More satyr in the groaning wood

And lured down on me hordes of souls, likewise
Concealed in horns and hooves,

Who ended me. What blinded my two piercing
Eyes that meant to see?

3. TEACHER

My gray eyes frisked your Earth for three things only—
The lean bodies of smart young men, true poems,
Sunlight.
      My body lived for bountiful meals
(Larded but zesty), reliable booze and the glide
Of my fingers on willing skin—those lean boys
Poised in the blocks of manhood: hungry to start
As I to touch, as godly as smart.
                    I dreamed
They watched in self-possessed thanks while my
Soft hands repaid their patient condescension
With skittish but, most nights, foolproof speed.
                        Three
Lay back; all but one of them watched in what I dreamed
Was mild forbearance, courtesy at least.
                      One
Of the watchers left my bed and blew his brains
Out five hours later. The other two ate my hearty
Cooking, drank my wine, graduated
And never looked back—not at me.

                  So I took
My hope to the fountainhead—Greek islands burnt
By a sun that gilds the occasional goatherd into one more
Snack for Phoebus, Zeus Himself, men wise
As Socrates: boys rare enough to carve and worship
Till stone, and the human race, dissolve.
                    Somewhere
Aging still above ground, my stack of dog-eared
Polaroids bears witness to what precisely I got
For the odd cigarette-lighter, cufflinks, dinner—these swart
Ephebes (goatherds turned sailor turned soldier, barely
Able to say the word *thanks*, if thanks had dawned
In heads as blank as their marble kin),
The dull percussion of honey-brown flanks on my
White ass and the sweet delusion of hearing the sear

Of their rank seed hurl into my waste. I never
Heard

       But ricocheted home in the nick of time
To pitch my slack white skin at the moil of a quick
Decade of risky dreamers, famished as me
And stripped to feed—more teachers, truckers, husbands,
Sailors, felons, horse-hung saints.
                      In white
Tile baths, I huddled on my hands and knees
While upwards of a hundred starvelings
Sowed their tribes of nonexistent sons
And daughters up my bore; then sowed my death—
A wilder famine, baby-new and cruel
As any madman's prayer.
                 From here at last
I see a fact I overlooked. *In fifty-*
Five ravenous years on Earth, no one I dreamed
Or touched or housed in my hot vent—no god
Or poet, man or boy—exceeded me
In the unstanched offer of an ample soul, full
Of unspent love as your average dad with silent
Woe. Neither death nor the fuming pit itself
Has canceled such a boundless gift, still
Unclaimed.
          Can any man I dreamed or pleasured—
Any boy I led into the steady sun—Art's
Courtly games of calm attention, perfect
Service, journey's ease—will any dare
This thick dark now and thank my barren burning
Hand?

HALF OF LIFE

With yellow pears
And full of wild roses,
The land hangs to the lake—
Auspicious swans—
And drunk on kisses
You dip your head
In holy sobering water.

But where shall I take, when
It's winter, the flowers and where
The sunshine
And shadows of Earth?
The walls stand
Speechless and cold; in wind
Cocks clatter.

after Hölderlin

THE EEL

1. 25 JULY 1984

Mother, the name of this thing is the eel.
It is one foot long, thick as a pencil
And lives in the upper half of my spine—
Ambitious now to grow all ways.
Every atom of me it turns to it
Is me consumed.

                    Yet it's been here always,
Original part—which is my first news
For you in years. It came in the first
Two cells of me, a gift therefore
From you or Father—my secret twin
Through those hard years that threatened desolation
But found rescue in dumb resort
To inner company, a final friend
Concealed at the core on which I'd press
Companionship, brief cries for help.

It helped. My purple baby convulsions
That got more notice than a four-car wreck,
Weak arms that balked a playground career
And kept me in for books and art,
Toilet mishaps, occasional blanks—
Tidy gifts to aim and guide me.
I steadily thanked it and on we came,
Paired for service fifty years.

Now it means to be me. And has made huge gains.
I'm numb as brass over one and a half legs,
All my upper back, groin, now my scalp;
Both arms are cringing weaker today,
And I walk like a stove-up hobo at dawn.

What broke the bond, the life-in-life
That saw us both through so much good?

Mother of us both, you left here
Nineteen years ago—your own brain
Drowning itself, eager blood—
And prayers to the dead are not my line;
But a question then: have you learned a way,
There where you watch, to help me kill
This first wombmate; strangle, fire out
Every trace of one more heirloom
Grinding jaws? Do you choose me to live?

Struggle to tell.

2. 26 JULY 1984

Mother, this man is now all eel.
Each morning he's hauled upright to a chair
And sits all day by a window near trees.
Pale leafshine honors the green of his skin,
The black-bead eyes. He wants no more;
His final triumph strokes him with permanent
Fuel for the years of wait, twitched
Only by drafts, damp rubs by his nurse
Or mild waves of gravity flushing the compact
Waste from his bore.

                       He does not know you
Nor the twin he ate. He could not name
The taste of joy, but he licks it slowly
In his bone hook-jaws. He thinks only "Me.
I became all me."

3. 26–30 JULY 1984

Mother, this man will stay a man.
He knows it three ways. First, he's watched
A credible vision—no dream rigged for comfort
But a visible act in a palpable place
Where Jesus washed and healed his wound,
The old eel sluiced out harmless in the lake.

   Then a woman he trusts like a high stone wall
Phoned to say "You will not die.
You'll live and work to a ripe old age"—
And quoted Psalm 91's reckless vow,
He will give his angels charge over you
To guard you in all your ways.

   Then he knows what a weight of goods rests in him,
The stocked warehouses of fifty-one years—
Waiting for export, barter, gift:
Lucid poems of fate and grace,
Novels like patient hands through the maze,
Honest memories of his own ruins and pleasures
(All human, though many blind and cruel).

Years more to teach the famished children
Rising each spring like throats of flowers,
Asking for proof that life is literally
Viable in time.
                    Long years more
To use what I think I finally glimpse—
The steady means of daily love
In daily life: the patience, trust,
Suspended fear, to choose one soul
And stand nearby and say "Be you.
Be near but *you*."
                    And thereby praise,
Thank, recompense the mind of God
That sent me, Mother, through straits of your
Own hectic womb and into life

To fight this hardest battle now—
A man upright and free to give,
In desperate need.

SIX CONSOLATIONS

1. AUGUST 1939

You drift on the creaky green porch swing and count
Dim water stains on the ceiling. They've dried themselves
Into maps of countries, shapes of organs—kidneys,
Hearts, Bolivia, lungs. The woman you
Trust best on Earth is snoozing not four feet
Away; you think her dream concerns your eyes,
Though you know she tried to kill herself two years
Ago—she has you now and means to stay
And said as much in ten plain words an hour
Ago. In another minute you'll think her name—
Not speak, think. Slow, the thought will lift
Her head. She'll turn your way and yawn and ask
"A brown-sugar sandwich or a cold fresh orange?—say which.
Quick, *say*." You mull the choice and think your entire
Drift, here out, will move this slow.

2. JULY 1946

Your mind has been continuous each step of the way,
Each day of more than four thousand days
Since you saw day. It keeps the sight of every
Gift you've won, each dread. Time was, it hauled
Dreads up by night to balk your rest. But here
Below, unbroken downward from that mind,
Your old child's body undergoes the greening
Upward flush of spring until one dusk
You understand your mind has built you one
Stupendous pleasure palace—stocked and humming,
Ready, free. You close your door and open
Both the windows on an evening lit
By fireflies burning their own substance, lone
As you. You shed your cotton summer clothes,
Lie full-length on the ample bed and wait.

3. JULY 1956

Midsummer late in Stockholm, hot, we hear
The birds complain—ingrates, barred from sleep
This near midnight by a radium glow: the sun
Half-tucked beneath that line of hemlocks, itching
To rise in four quick hours on town, lagoon,
The sea, the luckless herring, our rented room
Not half a mile from Garbo's grim birthplace.
We're not a minute past our own refusal
Of the world's raw gaze, our try at melding bodies
Fired by this uncanny light to pour.
I think *I'll take this moment, clear, to my grave*
And turn to give a penny for your thought;
But one more time you give it recklessly,
I doubt we'll spend this short a night again.
You sleep. I'll wait for day. Cool now, we wait.

4. SEPTEMBER 1961

You've had a long lunch at the Lamb and Flag with your old
Teacher and laughed full-tilt through everything
From British naval slang and trench warfare
(He fought in France, whiffed mustard gas) to the eerie
Chords of late Shakespeare—lost daughters found,
Cold wounds annealed. You've both skirted the week's
Bad news—Khrushchev's H-bombs stacked to your right
In split Berlin; Kennedy's glistening lockjawed
Moxie, cocked to lunge. You're still theoretically
Draftable, if America lasts to crank a draft.
Christ Church Meadow, your slow route home in glare
And shade, has never looked calmer, splodged with late flowers
And a tall girl singing in Gaelic to the sky.
You think *Any instant, this vaporizes.* Your teacher
Says "It's far too fine to vanish—say so."

5. OCTOBER 1976

We've weathered that *tsunami* of a day I still
Recall as my main day—the riverrun, a late
Long juncture—and here, next afternoon, we climb
The perpendicular laurel shag of the nearest
Peak, hospitable Hokum with her promised look
(In such pure air) right round the globe to at least
Japan: Kyoto, the flammable Gold Pavilion,
Black sand scored for meditation and a single
Fading bass gong tone. There—intact,
Though bushed and dazed—we only see the curved
Pacific, placid as silver every way
And not one other soul in view, even
On the beach a quarter-mile down. I say "I wish
We two survived alone in a planet painlessly
Cleared." You take your time and say "We do."

6. NOVEMBER 1989

Brown leaves gag the plucky creek. A last
Flamboyant lotus hangs, neck wrung by frost
This dawn—first kill. Fall, your next-least welcome
Stretch, stalking horse for curt black weeks,
The mind's black dog. But sun, this sudden ladder
Thrown across my legs and outward, one
Hot fling to the pond. Then crows, three gangsters strut
Through the ailing beech they've seized. And quick, I know
The only news of this dry day, the ending
Year—I'm needless. Bare. In which case, earnest
Bows to the day, in lieu of thanks to the unmoved
Mover that rolled me here, end-time, and left
Me needing food, light, water (*substances*,
Not symbols for the tawn of skin, understanding,
Purity). Needless, trapped and dying glad.

INITIATION

Whoever you are, walk from your room,
Which you now know, into evening.
Your house is the last before space,
   Whoever you are.
Raise tired eyes from your worn threshold
And slowly set a single black tree
Against the sky—slender, alone.
   You have made the world.
Huge, it ripens in silence like a word.
Then when your will has comprehended essence,
Shut your eyes. Gratefully abandon it.

after Rilke

MORTAL SEVEN

1. PRIDE AND SLOTH: 1985

Man of sorrows, grief's companion—
I am the man that suffers and am here,
No instant free of agony sufficient
To crystallize black coal to quartz.

Step closer now. I welcome touch.
This youthful skin—apparent standard
Human gear—muffles a steady
Feral moan, pain's harmony.

See, no fear. I welcome a chance
To spread my wound again, for you—
The single show of pure forbearance:
A man assailed to death but *here*

By his brute force, his will to serve.
Thrust in this slit. A pounding heart.

2. ENVY AND COVETOUSNESS: 1952

All you had that I wanted was you,
Not to taste your body but be it.
Wanted? There were maybe twenty nights
When I hid in shrubs beneath your window,
Hearing you laugh with your freshman roommate—
Baritone joy that made me not only
Dream (lurid color) of being you but
Crave it, waking, with a metal roar.

Did you ever guess? Did I fly one clue?
That summer we spent three nights together
Watching two dozen undoubted mammals
Prance for the crown of State Beauty Queen.
Who there saw how, dark at your left side,
I burned—corroded—to be mild you?

3. ANGER: 1985

None, a thoroughly puzzling lack.
Doctors, friends, commend it to me—
Excavate this smothered rage;
Bawl at the ludicrous rubber legs.

I've dug a long year—no glistening seam
Of anthracite to stoke the wail.

No diamond either, no joy in the dig.
Amazement maybe. A bystander's transfixed
Gaze at the debris, pride in a skill
I'd never suspected—models of the U.S.
Capitol dome in dry toothpicks,
No drop of glue: freak labor
In the yellow grin of death. But anger?
None. I'm entertained.

4. LUST AND GREED: 1962

We stroke through dry woods to this hid clearing,
Silently stand—eyes locked on eyes—
And strip to the last discardable layer,
Two hides laced with potable blood.

I break at the knees—a hinged boy-puppet—
And grazing your shins, begin to eat
You in hot red gobbets. You
Beg the service, yield with moans

Of responsive joy till—an hour of peeping
Birds overhead, the reservoir chuckling
Unseen beyond us—I pause and lean
To see you gone, consumed, *in me.*

Now I must stand, find the house, your wife;
Explain our lateness, disgorge your parts.

WINTER

Emblems of fall—vanishing, then vanished:
Fallen, rotten, locked in crystal cold.
The field is blank; the tree that once stood bold
Is torn by wind, though calmed at night by rain.

As I am calmed who rest now at the close,
Hearing the year's last question to the sky,
Hearing no answer to the rising Why?
Trusting an answer when spring's coming shows.

after Hölderlin

TWO SONGS FOR JAMES TAYLOR

1. HYMN

Source of all we hope or dread—
Sheepdog, jackal, rattler, swan—
We hunt your face and long to trust
That your hid mouth will say again
"Let there be light," a new clear day.

But when we thirst in this dry night,
We drink from hot wells poisoned with
The blood of children. And when we strain
To hear a steady homing beam,
Our ears are balked by stifled moans
And howls of desolation from
The throats of sisters, brothers, wild men
Clawing at the gates for bread.

Even our own feeble hands
Ache to seize the crown you wear
And work our private havoc through
The known and unknown lands of space.

Absolute in flame beyond us—
Seed and source of dark and day—
Maker whom we beg to be
Our mother, father, comrade, mate
Till our few atoms blow to dust
Or form again in wiser lives
Or find your face and hear our names
In your calm voice, the end of dark
If dark may end.

    Wellspring, goal
Of dark and day—be here, be now.

2. DAWN (JOHN 21)

After he died that dreadful way,
His friends gave up, went home to stay—
Wives and children, boats and fish,
Any way on Earth to drown the wish
To see his burning face again
And hear his voice flame through a night
That has them drifting now, half-lost
On a lake they fished the whole slow time
Till he walked by three years ago
And hauled them up to light and life,
Then bled in public view and died
That dreadful way—strip-naked,
Pierced: head, hands, feet, side.

Dead—darkest hour of any night,
When daylight stalls below the brink.
Seven friends in a bantam boat
Taste each other's hopeless hope.

Then light, serene, a fragile glow
Beyond them on the narrow strand—
A man upright in clothes so white
They race the sun to crow the day.

The man looks their way, cups both hands
And begs for food—"Boys, what to eat?"
When one shouts "Nothing, not one fish,"
He points to starboard—"Cast again."

They cast and haul the biggest catch
Of their whole lives; and then they search
The shadowed face of their new guide,
But one—the youngest boy, named John—
Sees the feet beyond them on
The narrow strand: naked, pierced,
Rusty, cold. John dares to cry

His hopeless hope—"Lord, Lord, Lord,
It's him again!"
                              Sick with glee.
Old crazy Peter hits the lake
And swims for land.
                              The others sail
A final hundred yards and beach
The teeming net, then edge ahead
To where the man waits, Peter gasping
At his feet.
                    They do not dare
To call his name. They do not touch
His rusty hands. But all their hearts
Are hot as if they'd feasted on
Warm new-baked bread and sweet young fish.

Then they smell his own big catch,
Broiling on a well-laid fire.
He's been here, waiting out the night—
For them, for them, they dare to hope.

With that whole teeming net behind them—
Food for all their kids and wives—
They hunker down in cool spring dawn,
No single word in all their mouths,
And wait again round this same man
Who claimed to love them from the start
And now has cut a way back here
With ruined hands through agony—
And three days dead—to prove his word
And feed them fish and bread again:
New bread from Heaven, fish from God.

DREAM ELEPHANTS

Huger than dreadnoughts, battleship gray,
Wise as the tallest evergreen
And mild as all my gentle kin—
Though incontestable overlords
Of me and the low-slung world I watched—
They roamed my life from the year I was three
When Father took us to a two-ring circus;
And one old female lugged herself
With solemn patience and the will to please
Through a tired set of stunts: for me
As fresh as love on sight.
                              Before
She shuffled back to peanuts, straw
And ludicrous leg-irons, in a silent chime
I knew I'd met a needless soul
For that last room in my mind, crammed
With hungry parents, nameless fears.
    After the show we found her feeding,
And my hand stroked her crusty hide.
Her long-lashed right eye drank me in;
I watched her store me and knew I'd stay—
Instant inexplicable obsession.

With plentiful orphan dogs in town,
Rabbits, tidy snakes and goldfish,
Why choose the least convenient mammal,
Insatiable as forest fires and chancy
To tame?
              Gone as I was,
From that glad night, I drew and painted them,
Shelved their statues in herds by the bed
And gathered reams of textbook facts
(Their trunks can find a lost straight-pin

On a moonless night or uproot oaks;
Their minds are endless vaults for what
They see or feel, endure or love).
Their place in me was the calmest place,
The room to visit in wordless sorrow
Or the private joy of lonely days,
Tramping the local fields and pines
In mute refuge from the other two
I loved as much—the bottomless hearts
Of Father, Mother, watchful as spies.

Free at six to leave the house
On my own rounds, I haunted movies—
Elephant Boy, The Jungle Book.
At nine or ten I began nightly prayers,
Steady and stubborn as howls for food,
That someway I come to at dawn
Faced with all I'd ever need—
Free in the backyard, one grown elephant
Waiting for me.
        By then I partly
Knew what for—for me to worship,
My choice of a single godly outcrop
On the swarming world, a worthy magnet
For my awe and praise and, best,
A heart to comprehend the burning
Daily news I'd bring in a secret
Language we two shared: blank code
To others, a soothing cure for her
And me as we grew into one enormous
Mind that bridged our former solitudes
And drugged our pain.
        I was broiled in puberty
Before I quit the epic dreams
Of me and an august elephant steed—
My guide to every useful craft
And risky dare, the bravery
To wade through fools and traitors till

Heavy with deeds, we died together,
Which would be far off.

                    Long years after—
Past shoals of human guides and losers,
Shielded by nothing harder than hope—
A glimpse of elephants came like grace:
No question they are our tall masters,
Bound to graze their tan savannas
Ages past our dying out.

                    Now, and me hacked off
At the waist, they roam me night by night again.
In dreams as pure as our first love,
They find my bed—slow single-file,
Changed worse than me—and call me in our
Old dark tongue to turn their doom:
Stampeded, killed, chain-sawed and left
To rot beside their panicked young.
   In every dream my same right hand
Goes out to meet that dense familiar
Skin, now fragile as my palm;
And my grown voice warms to sing
The healing bass harmonic arc
They taught me when my mind was smooth.
   But night by night before I end
The vital phrase, my ruined partner
Groans, staggers, pitches down
And, soundless at my frozen feet,
Shrinks to a dusty handsized carcass—
A pygmy toy for that tame herd
Of statues lined above my bed,
Trunk coiled in final agony
That even I, their truest living
Human kin, can meet with nothing
Stronger than a speechless vow:
   Loved a lifetime, thanked each day,
Die in this cold certain solace—
Starving vengeance stalks my race

That, crazed, obliterated you—
In blood and dung for common greed—
Who willed us nothing worse than peace.

NOON REST, BEST DAY

Eagles common as cones in the trees,
Water hectic and plaited beneath us—
Water in Leonardo's notes:
Single medium of making, ruin.

Sovereign sunlight ladled on legs
Ample then to bear you all
A long fall night toward our accomplished
Joint in midair, shedding joy.

Sun on eight unknown companions
(Sapped as we on adjacent rocks)
Of our dawn mail-run up the wild Rogue
Nine years ago—you asleep at my hand,

Cocooned in trust; I weighing the day
On this dry tongue, a full life's best.

TWO

DAYS AND NIGHTS 2

A JOURNAL

In *The Laws of Ice* I published the first year's work from a journal of poems, 13 February 1984 to 14 February '85. From the start, my purpose was to save a few of the arresting encounters, memories and thoughts that otherwise vanish through the mind's wide slats. I set myself three main conditions—each poem must be as true as possible to its stimulus (no lies and even the dreams are faithful transcriptions), each must be as taut and lucid as I could make it, and none could be significantly changed past the day or two of its arrival. I was not conscious that in June, midway through the first year, I'd be ambushed by a physical devastation, though in retrospect it's clear that the poems knew it.

They kept a grim pace with the early months; then the impulse broke and most of 1985 went unrecorded. The present stretch started on 14 October 1985 and ran till 13 February 1990, six years past the first impulse. The early poems here inevitably fix on that private internal combat. If a reader perseveres through the self-absorption, rescue comes, then a gradual outward look again at the world and other creatures, many of whom recur from Part One.

As before, the lines are determined by stress, most often the old English count of four accents to the line, with an indefinite number of unaccented syllables. And again many poems volunteered as sonnets. Apparently no other common shape fosters the range of voices I need—from easy conversation to a trim elevation, no space for dead wood.

1. PRAISE

This stands for praise—
A book of days
Of frozen terror,
Scalded nights,
The horn of healing,
Tethered flights
To follow that
Tall muffled light:
Whatever name
It wills to bear.

2. AGAIN

Praise?—this mountain bursting my back,
Blundering out toward day and light
Through me, the space I've fought to hold—
Clear of pain, secure for rest:
One evening glide toward tranquil night?

Pain. Labor. The birth-throes of death—
Mine, for me. Selected by what
Or whom? Sent why?

The source and socket
Of end and start.

What else? *Praise.*

3. REX

Fourteen days at a dismal junction,
Forty-two meals at the All-You-Can-Eat
Buffet and Grill (obese Gold Agers
Burdened with platters of strangled catfish),
No liquor, no unblotched skin to touch—

Yet I leave, reluctant. Your actual face,
Frank miracle, your pillared throat—
Ample abutment to bear a mind
That in dark eyes burns steady,
Grave, extending gifts: constant you.

4. THE DREAM OF SALT

I'm waiting for Jesus in a room built of salt,
I have an appointment; he's bound to appear.
But I stand now, studying the white walls round me—
Twenty feet high from a circular floor
And sheered in perfect hard-lined planes.
No one waits with me; I'm forced to stand
(No bench in sight). I'm calm, convinced
My wait will yield uncounted good.
I think one thought continually—
"Don't weep. One tear would melt this room."
Happiness floods me and I pour great tears.

5. NOCTURNE FOR A WEDDING, 26 OCTOBER 1985

Let there be night,
Your night at last—
Sworn man and wife.

Let silence be
Your single sheet—
The rest be flesh.

Let joy commence—
Grave rush between you—
Now for good,

Hallowed two—
Watched, loved by me.

6. THE DREAM OF FALLING

No jeweled hummingbird, no angel
Equals (much less passes) me.
I hang midair in a dim cathedral,
Poring slowly down faces of windows
Lit by setting sun outside—
Enormous roses, apostles, crowns;
A thousand tints of violet, green;
Then the face of God.

                       I prowl its hair,
Planes of a forehead prairie-wide;
Then dip past the cataract nose and lip.

The mouth springs open, an endless hole
That swallows me—the grandest bird.
I plunge down a throat more gorgeous than glass,
A luge-run paved in Byzantine mosaic,
Billion translucent gilded tiles—
All joy till I comprehend the goal,
Terminus waiting at Time's own end:
The heart of God, God's belly and vent.
Whelmed, doomed, I pray to stop.

No answer. *On.*

7. BEN LONG'S DRAWING OF ME

This face, serene as an anchorite's,
Is apparently mine—all friends name it.
Have I won nirvana unbeknownst?

At the least I've transmigrated you—
Broadcast these intrinsic lines
Behind your eyes, through the mind, down arms

To five blunt fingers that print me here:
The Long translation of my long text.

8. 31 DECEMBER 1985 (TO R.L.C.)

Even a sane man staggers to points where
The smallest grain may suddenly blast out
Promise or threat—the wrong birdcall,
The rate of sunlight prowling a face,
The day's first word. Today, butt-end
Of an endless year, you tumble me
From chair to car in chill sunlight
And then yell "Whoa!" I crouch in the plush,
Expecting blood—cut forehead, cut foot
(The practical hemophilia of the numb).

You've found, at your own safe feet in leaves,
My grandmother's wide gold wedding-band,
Century-old companion of her life
From marriage at sixteen to death at forty-eight
(Eight children, a flagging fame for laughter)—
Lost from my left hand days ago,
Despaired of till now. I seize it, cold,
And warm it fast on a stout right finger
Blasted by luck—a year redeemed,
Her fame renewed, her gift of time.

9. THICKET

Gone a week, your memory
Hardens in odd dim corners
Till a small assembly of statues
Halts where you once moved—
Thicket of perfect likenesses
Made merely from empty air,
Your force (eyes, mainly eyes),
And these two molding hands:
Brute longing, wild regret.

10. SAMUEL BARBER (1910–1981)

Sam, meaner than a lovelorn yellowjacket,
Twice as toxic—fanning me on
That first summer of my drunk first success
To climb a body given you in trust;
A barely human soul built of light
And foul him, claw him, burn him to his knees—

You're safe years dead and I'm bound safe
In this bolt-upright cripple's chair
To hear you out these twenty minutes.
First Symphony, one breathless reach,
You young as the me I let you spoil—
An angel's sunset amble through pines
Toward pure blind union, God's bald face,
Your just deserts.

11. STEPHEN SPENDER

Stephen, assailed at your new height,
Wreathed in hair like Everest's banner
Or the Jungfrau's struck by ice at dawn—
Remember this in this new storm:

Fifty-three years of kin, friends, loves
Have swept through, under, and past me—gone.
You've stayed, unblinking as my two eyes
And thanked in words more constant than we.

12. VALENTINE. HERON.

Mid-February, pond laced at the rim;
You chime one more year frozen shut,
Locked behind us—
                    lilac heron
Old as the pines that shade your shallows,
My famished grateful counting eyes.

13. NEAR A MILESTONE (FIFTY-THIRD BIRTHDAY)

Time is clearly no concern of the Great Watchmaker—
Keats, Mozart, Schubert, Anne Frank, James Dean;

My father strangled at a hale fifty-four,
Still working the ground at his feet (sweet laughter);

Me jackhammering my slow path, micron by micron
Toward my own dread: his early ghastly howling end.

14. PAID

Ten nights ago in a hospital bed
More like a pine box than most human constructs,
I lay in unblinking glare of pain
At four a.m. and asked if agony—
A late surprise—was worth donating
Toward our retirement of Christ's
Big loan, that hungry debt?

15. GOOD FRIDAY

Or gift. Is pain an outright gift?
Is he so far gone (three-quarter million days)
That pain sufficient to polish steel
Is his one memory of human form?—
Three hours of a stormy spring afternoon,
Spiked up in a reeking suburban landfill
To drain in sight of his toothless mother,
Her younger friends: clear in his mind
Still and wished back on us, last possible link?

16. EASTER SUNDAY 1986 (TO E.R.)

Permitted to write on this one Sunday
Of all the year, I roll these two
Uncertain hands (cold, twitching)
Into flat frank sun, face east and draw
The day's best sight—concave planes,
Hid valleys, hot wells (two walnut eyes):
Your resting face, consuming light.

17. BACK

A whole quarter's silence—
Flesh-colored tunnel with sanguine walls,
No time to speak of pain or fear,
No extra breath (and no real
Fear: fear is the luxury
Two years behind me,
A bourgeois comfort like overstuffed chairs
Or flannel sheets and pain
More nearly a bore today
Than the acid agony that blanked all March).
So *life*, an apparent road ahead
With what seem trees and sky for walls
And natural light. So work. So this.

18. AT SEA (TO E.R.P.)

Mother, this sea—narrow wedge
Of south Atlantic (gray sand, gray breakers)
And you born inland (red hills, black pines)—
Was your best element all your days.
Your face, ready smiler, beamed outrageous
At the whiff of brine twenty miles up the road.
But here—in shorts, heels on the rail
Of the southward porch, nothing between you
And white Antarctica but brine, brine—
You burned a grin fit to toast all penguins
Otherwise frozen in their crisp opera suits.

19. SKY, DARK (TO E.R.P.)

This sun, that raised your entire skin
To the winey pitch of Cordovan hides,
Would flatten me with papules, welts
(Skin loathsome as any scapegoat's driven
Dead Seaward with pustular welts and boils).

Now you wait out your twenty-second year
In tepid velvet grave-deep dark—
Your leather lips still curled in a rictus—
And I still huddle up here, surviving
In the safe cool shade of memory and eaves.

20. TWO CAVES, A HOUSE, A GARDEN, A TOMB (MEMORIES OF ISRAEL AND THE WEST BANK WITH J.C.A., 1980)

1. *Nazareth, Mary's house*

This mid-sized hill town, then a crossroads hamlet,
Has two sites of interest to show—a spring
From which all ancient residents drank and a cave
Covered by a vast bizarre modern church.
    For a Westerner, caves are strange but proper here—
Emblem of woman: dim convex force.

This one's Mary's house and has been so honored
Since at least the second century—small, low, shallow
With a marble altar saying *Here the Word Was Made Flesh,*
That hilarious unthinkable moment when virgin God
Merely boarded a spotless likely-teenaged girl
And spoke some sound, known only to her (she'd already
Agreed), and thereby flooded her darkest space
With scalding light—her eventual death, our torturing shine.

2. Bethlehem, birthplace

The birth cave of Jesus, plated in Byzantine glory
By Constantine, stands in the cliff-edge of this old village—
Birthplace of David a thousand years back. So no one
Can prove that the silver star—*Here Jesus Christ
Was Born of the Virgin Mary*—doesn't hang in air
Above David's birthplace or circumcision site
Or the very spot where Samuel stood, anointing
David (Jesse's baby boy) as Yahweh's choice,
Israel's next king and heart's delight:
For he was ruddy and had beautiful eyes.
                                              So
David bowed to Samuel's oil and drove Saul wild
To be surpassed by a shepherd boy born here,
Let's say, maybe ten feet down from a subsequent crib
    Which by then was the stable of a packed-out inn.

3. Capernaum, Peter's house

At our feet fairly certainly, Simon Peter's house—
A basalt ground-plan smaller than a burnt-out trailer,
Three cramped rooms in which Peter the Rock
(Dumb and lunging and a lot less faithful than a wet
Retriever), Peter's wife, her mother, maybe their children
Offered their mud-and-wattle roof to a man
From the next county west through the Horns of Hattin,
Deep notch clove in the lilac hills,
Because the man extended plain hope: "a fisher
For men!" when lately Peter and Andrew his brother
Had netted far more water than perch, the Peter's
Perch we ate that night, so fine, at our inn
Ten miles south—Tiberias, where Salome danced.

Here dozens of sick were met head on and entirely healed.

4. *Gethsemane, garden*

This urgent land
Is one huge rock—

Exultant rock,
Cold black terror:

David dancing nude by the Ark,
Christ sweating blood to dodge his fate,

All on this one rough-hewn slab
Extruded here, altar of one more sheltering church

Where Jesus, abandoned in dark, face down
Begged to live a human life

Not gashed, stove, pierced
And drained blue-white

But sustained upright with hope and voice.
Midday tomorrow he'll die—bald agony.

5. Jerusalem, Jesus' sepulcher

This warm cube, size of a diva's steamer trunk,
Has triggered Crusader and Saracen bloodbaths
The equal of several dozen Vietnamese tunnel-hives and canebrakes,
Though now is mopped dry and buffed by hungry hands
To a mirror gleam—my own slim face stares back
From the shelf that bore dead Jesus Friday dusk
To Sunday dawn:
                my face and neck in plea
For hope, life, long years of time when
Here I also bring my own big riddle—
Death, life, naked incalculable wait between.
   Hid in the three-foot cord of my spine
Is a foot-long tumor (*astrocytoma,* dark
Slick eel there with me from birth).
                     One spasm
Now in this hot cube might kill me on the floor.

6. *Mount of Olives, rock of the ascension*

There's a small rock (size of a year-old baby)
And in it, the deep print of what's undeniably
A man-shaped foot—the down-thrust of Jesus
As he jetted skyward, a man-carved joke
Or shameless fraud or natural accident?
Too late to know. This plain dome at least
Has shielded the print from its destination—
Maybe endless sky—since sometime before 392.

We're here alone. The Arab child,
Whose key let us in, is back outside
Playing hopscotch with raucous friends.

You say "Look. This could be my last appearance,"
Then shuck your shoe and set your huge
Right foot in the print.
                              And stay with me.

21. A HERON, A DEER—A SINGLE DAY

A dull tin noon and, struck down on us
From the crest of pines, a heron—the one
That's brought me each winter solstice
For twenty-six years now whatever code
I've earned for the past year, need for the next:
Vast as a stork in a child's old reader
And fierce in the head as a demon deputed
To pluck out human eyes in vengeance,
Bolt them down hot.
                                    Yet our two faces
Broaden—eased, assured once more
Of witness at least: our names and precise
Address still known to Guidance Central.

Midnight mist and roaring cold,
We roll toward home from Christmas-eve dinner;
And there in the glen, frozen at the verge,
A six-point buck, young in eye
And grace of joint but flat-eternal
In steady witness. We slow to spare him—
Or think to spare a soulless thing.

He spares us. Sustaining our glare
A long instant of still composure,
His eyes consume whatever we show.
Then in a solemn choice to leave,
He melts a huge body, graceful as girls,
Through two strands of vicious barbed-wire.

We pass unscathed, drive in silence
A last slow mile, then both laugh sudden
At the sight of home. *Seen*, well-seen
But spared to pass.

22. FIRST GREEN

All ancient hopes are not, by nature, lies.
The dream of green does not preclude new leaves.

The fact that here in drystick winter
We long for spring, new life on limbs,
Does not mean spring will not transpire.

That intricate all-but-smoke of green
On the smallest trees at the riverbank
(Their upmost hands) is only the billionth
Promise paid—resurrection,

Frank hint of endless rounds in steady light.

23. 15 MARCH 1987 (TO W.S.P.)

Today I've lived my father's life—
Fifty-four years, forty-two days.

Father—there beyond that wall—
I beg to pass you, beg your plea

For excess life: more earthly luck
Or a longer sentence in the old appalling

Gorgeous jail in which you craved
My vivid mother, made my bones.

24. 16 MARCH 1987 (TO W.S.P.)

Given. Today I exceed your life
By an extra day of gray warm rain;

And there just now through glass on the air,
My heron soars in to work the pond—

"Symbol of longevity" here this year
Long past his usual winter stay

Despite two snows and his mythic age:
Tall slate-blue spirit, never leave.

25. SPRING TAKES THE HOMEPLACE

A long wet winter since I saw the house
Pounded hard by August sun—
Choked in stands of waist-high grass,
The lumber scrap of renovation—
And even now, all I have is pictures:
A cousin's color-snaps last fall.
The grass is scythed, the scrap hauled off,
The view from the window where I saw light
That bleak first day is clear again—
Straight sight to the road I took to leave
More or less for good, barring childhood visits
To Ida, not the place (Aunt Ida, saint
Of my saint-strewn life).
                       It's stood through
Three snows, hard sleet, the quick reversal
Of a ten-year drought—empty still,
No tenant yet. At least I've heard
No word of fire; so it must stand
Or crouch (*crouch* or *lie?*)—snoozing snake
Laid on the long lot, digesting its century
Of food: our lives (Rodwells, Drakes,
Prices, Rowans, Huffmans, Swifts).

None of us there to meet the spring,
Throw the doors wide on green-gold light
And acknowledge the silent service of walls,
A good tin-roof, and heart-pine floors
Through hateful cold.
                    So from this distance—
Eighty miles—I grant its virtue,
Grant our thanks (living and dead).
And these eyes roam the yard in memory,
Hunting a bloom to deck the door.

Ida's roses were long since blighted
To thorny sticks, razed and burned;

The rows of annuals long since a wilderness;
Only the tall old fig survives—
Backed against Buck Thompson's shed
(Where he stored the coffins he sold, a sideline
With sweet potatoes and brightleaf tobacco).

Life creeps up dry spongy pith
Of limbs that still bear pounds of figs
For cardinals now or cocky jays,
The sticky milk of ancient sap—
Loyal, punctual, undeterred.
No leaves yet, no fruit till August.

But from here, in mind, I break a stick;
Wait for the sweet milk; smear my hand
With its proof of lasting, in a long straight line
(Opalescent, warm in the cool day);
Bear that to the front door, press the hand
To a brass knob turned by all my kin
Through a hundred years. The door breaks open
At last.
            Spring light! Now rush on past me.
Flood the rooms.

26. THE RESIDENT HERON

Twenty-eight years this pond was visited
Briefly near the winter solstice by a Great Blue
Heron tall as a boy and famished
As sand, a single bird distinguished by a growth
On the back-folding joint of one of its legs.

A month early this year, my eye caught a flurry
In the yard well beyond me, the lilac rush
Of something fairly enormous landing. When the image
Resolved itself, there stood the heron—
A heron, these legs were healthy and taller than before.

He stood in the gravel drive sideways to me
Long enough to let me learn his presence and frame
The questions he plainly set—is he mine
(My old bird healed and bigger now as he nears
His thirties) or am I his? If the latter,

What next? Then in the slowest motion, he triggered
The awful process of levitating
Up and off—the twenty yards to the pond's
Deep end where, each day since, he's gorged
His flat blank face in my presence:

Apparently a resident, even this noon since—there,
In a hard sleet-storm—he stands, braving
Whatever short or lengthy trial fate has
In mind for the local livestock: me

And the few million more live forms he watches daily
As king, angel, ultimate judge or famished bird.

27. LIGHTS OUT (TO E.R.)

A whole day of sleet and just at dusk
The power fails. We're left to face
A frigid night with only the warmth
Of a squat woodstove for thirteen rooms

And I with a fever and all the hours
Of no way to read, watch a movie or type
(Sob for Fate's inveterate fool);
So I watch the jagged blade of an oil lamp

And try to mime the altitudinous
Thought of a monk winging a mind
Blank as ultimate Buddha at simply a wall.
An eon turns, I pass the first stars,

They vanish behind me. And home at dawn,
Even my name is unseen smoke.

28. THE RACK

Weeks of threshing the family photos,
Gleaning faces to feed a memoir—
I start each day expecting sadness:
The thousand captive grinning eyes,
Long since blind in red-clay graves.
   I find no fear on any mouth
But frank displays of a taste for time
As unassuaged as an alley drunk's
For dollar wine.
           To have watched each one,
From my own start, and now to set
Their secret down for a world to watch
And own and judge—*More life. Bring it on*:
A gift as big as any yet
From whatever unseen hand endows me
And stakes me too on the desert rack
That will parch me soon as dry as they—
A random ghost, all face, no voice
But maybe these lines.

29. JIM, WITH AIDS

Thirty years past, we were all but boys—
Full of ourselves as Christmas dinners
And ready to feed the world our bounty
Yet bound by a single ceaseless craving,
Beauty in all his licensed forms
And one illicit:
     Phosphorus flares
On the black horizon—music (a siren
Train of voices, vowing bliss),
The signal shine and pulse of verse
That also pledged safe harbor, rest
And the endless unpredictable faces,
Proffered and near, that we both worshiped
But only I reached toward and touched
And saw smile back.
      Now struck still,
I only watch—no reach, no touch—
While you, desolate as Lot's salt
Wife, are eaten in agonizing crumbs
By a fate more famished even
Than we.

30. TOM, DYING OF AIDS

In seven years you took my picture
A thousand times—in New York mainly
Ringed by gawkers, muggers, geeks—
And you as high as any bystander:
Lobbing me jokes like booby-trapped balls,
Tying your limbs in sheepshank knots
To break my pose and make me yield
Or asking me questions God will blush
To ask at Judgment. I'd laugh and answer;
You'd click and brush my hair aside
Or turn to a geek, "Ain't this boy
Fine?"

       I always came out
Looking like me. Others complained
(Nobody likes the you you like), but
You agreed—*It's you. I just* found *you.*

  Today I hear you're nearly lost,
Under a hundred pounds, eyes out,
Hid from all you saw and served.
  But Tom, I find you—see you still
In parks, up alleys, wrenching your face,
Your wiry limbs, into clowns and monkeys:
Finding *me.*

31. FISHERS

Mid-September noon—warm on the porch,
Reading the rowdy life of Saint Paul
(Our oldest lover, hottest scourge),
A killer hurricane grinding north
Eight hundred miles south and I as calm
As the pond beyond me, poised for a visit
From Monet at least: that posed and lilied.

And there a sudden heron lights,
Slow motion in the near-edge shallows
Thirty yards off.
                    Can he be the blue
Transformed crudescence that lit in the drive
Last winter, giant? No hint, no sound.
I freeze all the same to grant him ease.

Blue, yes—the lilac brown of rabbit fur;
But something here at this end repels him.
He lifts again—a jokey wonder
Of struts and flaps that would ground a flea
Yet buoys him from me, slow as he came
And at least as fine.

Is it me or some other lack he scorns?
If I knew, would I care? Could I move some way
To lure him back; could the world adjust
Its gilded, pocked and horrent hide
To earn his grandeur, grant him welcome?

Skip it. Eat this limpid air,
An early merciful autumn food.

First time in years, I barely ask
If my blue fisher trolls for me.
Today he seems a skittish bird—
Not more, none less, a freak of the light—
Creaky, cranky, good to see.

I wing a brisk thanks to the hole he's left
In the pond's dumb patience and return to Paul.

Paul, fierce dwarf! His brutal hand,
Relentless eye, fish the whole flat

Mare nostrum boiling with us,
Our scaly souls his tasty prey.
He'll stand and gaff us, love us briefly,
Then hand us up to the hungry sky.

32. YOM KIPPUR 1983–88 (TO D.S.V.)

Sundown a full five years ago,
We threaded streets in east Jerusalem,
Fumbling a way to the Wailing Wall
By hunch, no map.
                              Then sudden blood
Thick at our feet, the dim alley
Paved with blood fresh enough
To gum our shoes and rank with the iron
Stench of a massacre, minutes old.
    You found a sign, *Street of the Butchers*—
Flayed, gutted lambs in reach of our hands
(Three hundred maybe, blue as bruises)
And not one visible human in the stalls.
    All killed by me, I suddenly knew
And jogged ahead to claim my crime.

33. JIM DEAD OF AIDS AN HOUR
AGO, 25 SEPTEMBER 1988

Full moon on Earth, calm autumn night,
And word of your death in the telephone voice
Of a decent man you taught years back
Who saw you through.
                              Full moon, you cold
In warm Key West. Old slave of the sea
(You'd walk through fields of broken glass
For a smell of surf, its battering light),
The blind avenger that cored you out
And swamped your mind dies now with you,
Drowned in the final towering surge.

   Full moon, flood tide, drew you at last
To your best height. Death and victory—
The killer killed.
                              Sail far, kind
Ancient luckless boy.

34. TWO (TO D.L.)

Twenty-nine years of the Great Blue guest,
A clutch of poems to mark his descents,
Even his recent phoenix-change—
Entirely renewed, though lone as ever
Near a me companioned, me fitted with help
From my own kind: a steady soul,
Intent beside me, mind on me.
   And now cold noon, writing at the window,
The pond mud-yellow from last week's snow,
I catch the usual skirmish of blue.
Two Great Blues rise from the near deep end,
Foiling the laws of aerodynamics
One more time and clutching at air—
A second pair on the place, fed and flying.

35. EASTER SUNDAY 1989

Drollest day of the calendar year—
A battered corpse alive again,
Upright walking, to the consternation
Of a covey of former fair-weather friends,
Who gave a new meaning to "left in the lurch"
Last Thursday night. Yet here he's back
And with nail holes to prove it in the midst of a cold
Fish supper they've somehow managed to cook,
For all their gob-stopping shame and grief.
   Me, it's coming on evening here.
I've had a hot lamb lunch with cheesecake
Somber as strontium, and rolled outdoors
To the pondside deck, ready as ever
For my annual call from the Galvanized Stiff
Who made this universe at least,
If not zillions more, yet brings me too
The flabbergasting uproarious news—
You may, at will, companion me
Till Hell frosts over and countable time
Is swapped for endless alternations
Of light with restful dusk and angel
Serenades in earnest of utter safety,
Sure tranquil dawn.
             A slow
Warm hour of earthly twilight, the pond
Now still as a marble slab—the fish
All sink to early sleep; small birds
Jitter as ever near night, afraid
This dark will be the one stamped deep
In their hot brains, the dark that lasts:
No dawn, no food.
           And I wait too,
Calm to the passing eye but edgy,
No visit still.
         Then a streaking shadow
Blots my hands; I look straight up—

A hawk, fervent as any bullet,
Flings skyward through the failing day;
Takes the final western glare
And melts in my sight, melts for me.
    I let that be my manifestation
For one more year—my sign, proof,
Grounds for hope.
                                  What blistered child
Abandoned sleeping by his monster father
In desert scrub has more, has less?

36. TOM DEAD

More than a year of utter silence—
Stashed in a sister's merciful room,
You the mute black hole in its midst—
And now this word of a death that ate you,
Cell by cell to the livid bone;
Then sucked at the marrow till the mind, aghast,
Parched and shrank and shook in the skull:
Grit in a rattle, your final music,
Who for generous years in sight and hearing
Made a visible line of silent praise
From nothing but my own dying face
And the thousand other faces you played,
The thousand smiles you forced to light,
All dying with us but slower than you.

37. DOWN AND BACK

First hot spring day, humid as Delhi
And a muttering thunderhead on hand,
My two legs jitter like galvanized frogs—
Banging the baseboard, rocking the lamp.

I kill the phone, wheel to the sunporch
And play the eighteen-minute tape
Of my hypnotist's disembodied spiel—
Me in the clouds, then gyring down,

Then into the warm lake, through its murk
To the door in its deepest silt, then *down*
Till his sovereign voice commands my mind
To end its pointless self-torment

And oar back up to cooler light
With legs becalmed as bathtub boats
And the musky scuppernong globe in my mouth
Of sane return, a sober man.

38. THANKS

This fabulous loneliness dense as diamond, now my home.
This frozen thrilling air my lungs have learned to breathe.
These hands, serene as water birds, that know no need
To reach or take or love or kill.
                          All burn a silent
Praise of thanks to what or who has worked such peace.

39. SCANNED

The annual scan of my spinal cord
Took a long four hours a week ago,
And now my surgeon breaks a silence
That had started growing teeth and claws.

"Clean, *clear!* I'm more than glad;
You've outlived your old prognosis again.
Course, I'm convinced there's tumor there;
Convinced we'll have to deal with it yet—"

Laughing, I stop him and prompt the truth,
"You were sure I was dead five years
Ago." Now to keep him foiled
And glad—not, to be sure, entirely

My job.

40. THE NET

Five years since and I sit here winnowing
The hill of mail I got those burnt months
In '84. Then I could hardly
Force my eyes to see the lines
They flung toward me—hot protestations,
Hopes, vows—much less catch them.
   Now though, safe through one more gauntlet,
I haul them down at last, brace and read
Each—safe as stories. One stranger writes
"I've got a whole convent of nuns praying for you
And they get *results*."
              So, plainly, they did
And all the zealous rescue squad
That, flinging lines in near-pitch dark,
Managed unknown to weave this buoyant
Iron net I ride today.

41. *NEW MUSIC* IN CLEVELAND

Nothing but words tapped out in a room
While the merciless eel ascended, blind
But upward bound—my racing brain.

Five years on, the words and I
Are live at the edge of a poisoned Great Lake
That still, from this high window, at noon

Roils and foams with an ancient fury
It will not yield. Nor I nor those
Mere words that burn on strangers' tongues.

42. J.H.

Big-eyed and trusty as a Labrador—
Six years ago, I'd have stoked each cell
Of my dynamo to incandescence
And fined my aim at the one hid atom
In your broad mind that needed me
And would warm in my pure heat and pour
Your central private essence—food
For which, those years ago, I'd gladly
Have given my hoard of goods:
Nostrums, geegaws, rattles, flutes,
Sextants, talismans, torches, runes
And a deathless pledge.
                    Seated now
I shine this honest useless smile
That you shine back, respondent moon.

43. MOB QUAD, OCTOBER 1955

Thirty-four years ago this week,
You rapped on a medieval door,
Heard my "Come in" and took four steps
That entered my life.
                  No handshake, names
But within half a minute, I saw your secret—
Chill to the eye as the city round us,
You burned the constant self-fed light
I'd waited all my life to see;
And since I guessed I was your Balboa,
I rightly guessed you'd welcome and warm me.
   This far beyond, I watch you still
That autumn dusk; and in that light,
Still I bathe these empty hands.

44. AT HEAVEN'S GATE, MAY 1956

Tomorrow you pass your twenty-first birthday.
We'll drive with two carloads of friends
To Longleat House in the country near Bath
And sit on a hill called, understandably,
Heaven's Gate in frail sunlight
That nonetheless gilds each visible cell
Of your plentiful hair and makes you, not just
The birthday boy but the present goal
Of more eyes than mine—three horsefaced
English girls with double-cream skin,
A strapping stereotypical spinster
And six agreeably coltish Rhodes Scholars
Who frisk the sight and fact of you,
Coolly helpless as if they watched,
Say, Leonardo sketching curls
Of twining water in a turbid weir
While all gnaw chicken and drink cold cider,
Mindless that not one soul among us
Will ever know a finer day,

Though you and I built a finer night
Hours before, twining together—
Hot in a freezing room and bare
As gods exchanging ichor slowly
With rich side-dishes, celestial garnish
(No words, all thanks)—telling ourselves
In silent code that this thick dark,
This sage negotiated joy,
Would stay walled deep in our two minds;

And so it has, thirty-three years
(The span of Christ) till, here, I write
This plain recall, sharing at last
The secret huge exploit we dared

As you stood, frank, in the gate of manhood,
Meeting my gift with a full return
That's in me still: undiminished,
Food for life.

45. BOAR'S HILL, SPRING 1958

Trailed behind us the past two months,
That buried line of dark oases—
Bleak rented rooms in which we joined
To dowse for nurture and never failed:
Tresco, Compton, Oxford, Edinburgh,
St. Andrews, Cambridge—indoor wells
That quickly bred astounding foliage,
Shade and rest.
              But here at last,
A sunbaked Sunday, we lie in foot-deep
Grass in a clearing not more than a hundred
Yards uphill from the stately homes
Of culture princes—Gilbert Murray,
Bridges, Masefield, Arthur Evans
(Who found, then half-invented, Knossos).
We mean to read till dusk at least,
Then dine at the Tudor Cottage in Iffley
With maybe a dusky after-hour
In your dim room, ivy-hid.
    But the clean sun pounds its own intent;
And sworn as we are to work apart,
The merciless weight of curing light
Engorges both our starving skins
Till soon, obeying helplessly
And plain to see, we meet full-length—
Calm face to face—and through the screens
Of cotton, wool, we conjugate
In flagrant disregard of nearing
Human voices, laughing high.
    My first and only implication
In an act as common as outdoor mammals
And aimed at no iron lasting construct—
Life together, deathless love
(We've laughed them both well out of sight).
Yet here it burns, these cold years late,
To light a numbing autumn day—

The quarter-hour we burned through clothes
And our rash vows of levity:
Young and ready, grinning broadly,
Blind as blood but undismayed.

46. A HERON, A DEER—AGAIN

The two together in one more day—
Morning, a young and trusting doe
Materialized by the drive out front,
Unspooked by cars or us at the window
And gone as strange and quick as she came;
Toward dusk, the sudden slate-blue flash
Of a heron, broadside, climbing air:
All knees and elbows, immensely strong
And streaming awe, though awkward as any
Clambering kid.
                         Thirty-one years
Beside this pond, they and their
Progenitors have, at the least,
Registered me—a dazed smiler
Straining to read their bold recurrence,
The magnanimity with which they print
Their emblematic shapes on a world
That, year by year, compounds the warp
Of the trap it weaves to end them both
And all their kind.
                         Refuge, rescue,
Where to hide them, where's sweet water,
Fish, clean grass, deep woods and lakes
That rest unshook in natural bounds?
    Nowhere but this silent cube
Behind my eyes where, day by year,
I store the weight of the heavy grace
Of, at the least, these slots on tranquil
Blinding light—a bird, an elegant
Quadruped, glimpses of their normal
Daily hunt for food or usable
Upright phantoms of God, thrust
My way on land to which I hold
A deed these few quick years.

47. SPIRIT FLESH, 1960

Horn Branch, its homely pond, accept the snow.
Weeds and scrub hunker their winter crouch
This last gray week before the darkest day.

Same branch, same pond and these weeds' hardy forebears—
Three decades back we lay in summer dusk
And counted fish: their skittish leaps for bugs,

Their agate eyes. Still nothing we saw was half
As fine as we—our coal-black hair, our eyes,
Your seamless skin, pure and taut as a bolt

Of creamy silk. Just at dark a snapping
Turtle surfaced, big as a tub;
You named this *Turtle Spirit Pond*.

He's down there still, realer by the year.
We're here, still hot to yoke on this white page.

48. ANTIPODES, 1969 AND ON

Late summer, then fall, then six more years,
You took this skin (that had been no use
To another human for a long dry spell)
And paved it, plated it—scalp to heel—
With your frank need and the will to serve
Till I could pass myself again
In random mirrors and not recoil;
Till—night on night—I drank the view
Of your gray eyes consuming me,
Healed by the salt of our joined laughter.

49. FREE FUEL, BYRD STREET, 1948

Five days shy of the solstice, ice
Binds the pond, glazes my ramp
To a slalom chute; so back I skid
On forty-one summers to you and me.
Hot dark, twin beds, a sweephand clock,
A penlight to read it and our two scorching
Separate forks—panting for touch,
Though touched by nothing but our sealed selves—
Are pounding down the course we've set,
Come first, fling farthest, till each arrives.

Who won, remember? I know the time—
Forty-four seconds: we were both that green,
Both under sixteen and chocked with seed
As any silo west of Wichita.

No word of you since the early sixties—
Your first divorce, bourbon-soaked.
Still here we stretch indoors again
And stoke the coldest day all fall.

50. FIRST LOVE, HAYES BARTON, 1948

Your room was a short two blocks from mine,
Though straight uphill and the close equivalent
Of two light years. I'd never knocked,
Never said so much as a word to you;
And still I'd lurk on my cot by night,
Weaving a burning Nessus shirt—
The ways to make you, first, my friend
And then the naked mate to my skin:
   (Leave your window open late).
I'd offer my hefty savings account
(Take this, shut both your eyes, lie still,
Take me—this tidal surge of worship
I ache to pour down your tan length.
   Lave's the word for what I needed—
To lave you day and night with the honor
You'd more than won by your strong head,
Two eyes the shade of a desert zenith
High noon, midsummer, and a grin like dawn
On scalding night.
            Never—no hint
Of my dammed flood, though we laughed through sophomore
Latin class and senior P.E.
   Still—forty-one years—your Christmas card
Kindles the face you earned and gave:
Imperturbable tall Hermes,
The Guide of Souls.

51. ELEGY, BYRD STREET

Three days—two poems—ago, I wrote us down,
Pounding our racing bodies side by side
In August night and both triumphant. Three days

And here's the final word on you—your name,
A date—in our old school's newsletter: dead.
No explanation, fifty-two years old.

Of all my earnest mates then, first to go,
First to know how near our robust skin
Thrust toward the absolute ecstatic goal.

52. 1 JANUARY 1990

Clear New Year's day, a fresh decade,
Washed light and the sky a lidless ceiling;
But last night I woke at four

And, helpless, underwent the passing
Of a bitter grainy cloud, black loss—
The half-turned heads of all my *gone*:

The dead, offended, lunatic, fled
In anger, fear, self-entrapment,
Cold repulsion, paralyzed sloth.

A slow hour I worked to turn
One face my way, both eyes to mine.
Not one agreed; all took a last step

And vaporized. Up, this sterling day
Alone, I court the hurtling fickle sun—
Pale whore but free this noon and speechless.

53. SAFEKEEPING, 1963 AND ON

You again, back by night in an entertaining
Instructive dream—both of us
Young as in fact we were and locked
In one more run of our main event:
Using you, stretching your compact
Trunk and limbs, your dropdead face
And a soul as huge and helpless as Newark
On the Junglegyms of dare and danger
That always certified you fit
For every soul-depleting trial.

In this case here last night, you hunted
Chest-deep in the sumps of Hart Swamp—
Scenting, sighting cottonmouth moccasins
And gentler than both our mothers' hands,
Thrusting a deadly head my way;
Then returning the unharmed dragon
To its chosen tree as if its safety
Were crucial to the wheel of time
As yours was not.
                              Near three decades
Of liquor, wives, stunned kids, grinning
Leeches, your frank though glazed and bottomless
Thirst for poison—all I have's
Your phone voice maybe once a year
(Entirely itself, prodigal cello)
And here the face I find in dreams:
Prime of faces all my life,
Undeterred in radiance—mere fact
Still safe in my sole mind,
Your last refuge.

54. GIANT

Only this humming radiant boundary—
The band of light that hovers at his body
And seems another product of his sleep—
Defines the length of a frame that dwarfs the Urals.
Only a steady sigh of breathing moves;
Its cool mist feeds the riot of deep moss
That coats the floor and unseen walls of a cave
Where, unrecorded time ago, he chose
This ledge to start his urgent sleep and dream.

   Or are the cave, ledge, moss, the mist, the light
And that titanic body likewise dreams
Borne on a web of disembodied mind
That dreams and constantly creates our world
At least—the spinning furnace core of the farthest
Quasar, blackest hole, the lethal bow
Of hungry keen Orion, tender limbs
Of the Pleiades, you and me to the root
And every jigging universal atom?

   Or is our own giant folded in the sleep of some
Archaic dreamer (larger, smaller, past
Our power to think); and he in turn?—

                        The tale
I told myself at six years old when Hitler
Killed the children in his reach and reached for more,
While in a country suburb, lone as Lindbergh,
I trawled the woods and piney air for rescue—
Building a safer world at every glance:
The hectic trust that life described some logic,
Moved at the will of one tall smiling face.

   I couldn't know I'd innocently found
A thought almost as ancient as my sleeper,
Conceived and reconceived by priests and children,
And always balking at a final blank—
What happens to his world when the giant wakes?

       *

In my case, fifty-seven years of me
Have felt unbroken—seamless, good or bad,
Except the hours I lost to anesthesia
(Blackest of holes, no fear, no hope, no help)
And those rare nights when sleep herself becomes
A wordless thoughtless merciful black box.
    So I assume he dreams on undisturbed;
And since the boy who found him dreams in me—
The nest of Chinese boxes, each in each,
Where every model of my former selves
Dreams still—I move on now in wary courtesy
(Soft tread, no cries) in slim ferocious hope
No dreamer wakes.

55. MAYA

Found this note of Einstein's, late
In his life on an old friend's death—
                          This death
Signifies nothing. For us believing
Physicists, the distinction between past, present
And future is an illusion, even if a stubborn
One.

          In adolescence I wrote him
More than once—would he sign a portrait
Drawing I sent?
                    No answer then;
Now this old-man outright claim,
More useful.

56. 13 FEBRUARY 1984–90

This clean new wing of the house looks east;
So eyes, that match their wide selves
In photographs from '84,
Scan the pocket-pond I've scanned
These thirty-two years of human noon.
   Frequent sights of former me
Materialize by willows, coves—
Plain as the days I shucked them off,
Dry as snakeskins, faithful molds
Declining to fade—tall boy, lovesick
And proud of his wounds; eventual man,
Part-healed, still hunting.
               Is any actual
Atom left that spun in place,
Even six years past as I cranked these lines?—
Hardly in my salvaged frame, though
Maybe hid in the cores of rocks;
Thickest plate on the shell of the dozing
Turtle, my senior. Maybe far
Inside the heart of these numerous eager
Boys, my ghosts—assuming they lead
A hardy life beyond this mind
That sees them now, amazed in thanks,
While they wolf down their plentiful lot:
Young and way too dumb for fear.

THREE

JUNCTURE

In Book VIII of *Paradise Lost*, Adam and Eve entertain the
Archangel Raphael in Paradise. At the end of a pleasant luncheon
during which the angel tells too many secrets of Heaven and the
Universe, Adam tells the angel of his own erotic infatuation with
Eve. When Raphael warns of the dangers of abdicating reason,
Adam turns table and asks Raphael if the angels enjoy sexual rela-
tions like those that delight him so dangerously? Raphael blushes
and responds.

> *Whatever pure thou in the body enjoy'st*
> *(And pure thou wert created) we enjoy*
> *In eminence, and obstacle find none*
> *Of membrane, joint, or limb, exclusive bars:*
> *Easier than Air with Air, if Spirits embrace,*
> *Total they mix, Union of Pure with Pure*
> *Desiring; nor restrain'd conveyance need*
> *As Flesh to mix with Flesh, or Soul with Soul.*

Pure we were that late summer week
Ten years ago in the Land of Rain
So blessedly dry that, strong as we,
Light succeeded in finding our lives
Hid in the least of a ring of huts
That made a Mom and Mom motel—
Two husky owners (Mim and Dit),
Big laughers both with dutchboy bobs,
Yapper dogs, a first-rate kitchen,
Fake pond size of a wading pool
In which tired travelers fished their dinner,
Famished trout longing for the pan
(You dropped your hook; they struck like sharks)
And just the shaggy butt of Mount Hokum
Between our sleep and the ocean endlessly

Gloating beyond.
 Though we hadn't confessed it,
What we were after was finding the walls,
Nets, bars, traps, hooks
In both our minds that foiled the mute
Clandestine will, total mixture.

The second day you'd planned a trip
Up the Mad River in a mail-tourist launch—
Dawn as our flat hull spanked up the delta,
Struggling past unthinkable hemlocks,
Eagles thick as gnats on the boughs
And bald as Mount Shasta, pioneer wives
In aprons and grins avid for news.
 Lunch on a clutch of languid rocks;
You half-bare an arm's reach past me
On a private slab, amply rewarding
The sun with partial views of a form
Well-made as anything animate between
The southernmost cell of your pelt and the first
Live sequoia, all rings intact
With sabertooth clawmarks hid in the heart
(My thought, not yours who hardly knew
The point of a mirror). How did I nap?
You napped, I mimed exhaustion and followed.
 Cool afternoon, the rush downstream.

Safe back, drugged with calm, I flung
My slack bones prone on the broad bed
To sleep an hour of late gold air
Until you woke me with a rocking hand
On the nameless plane where vertebrae stop—
Your blue eyes the streaming core of the room,
All the rooms we'd warmed in six years:
Cornflower brands that signed a way,
Lights that hailed me on you from the start.
 I swam up ready at the silent call—
Silent because you'd never yet

Conceded the force that worked your eyes,
Hands and body: rank as roots
That shatter tombs through generations—
And found your determined face, astounded.
   You granted at last a hunger deep
As the parched moon's pull on the nutrient tide;
And you worked on slow but *worked* in time,
Disclosing me to the failing day,
Cherishing me with the grave obeisance
Of newborn creatures to their generous kin;
Then bearing down on me at angelic angles
More intricate, more deeply cut
On the air's dry plane than any meeting
In Euclid's dream of perfect juncture—
Mitred joints so true no chink
Of sun could pry.
              At the tall apex,
Open-eyed, I prowled the reaches
Of your whole mind—each muffled plan,
The throttled shames, pockets of joy
And dauntless trust—till in one broad
Eventual glide, I was all you,
You me, we single.
                An actual minute
In manmade glare so loud the walls
Refused to hold it, tossed it back
To baste our single glorious hide;
And then before the bond could part,
I rose on you and repaid the gift
With ample interest, a fortune earned—
Unshielded passage to all my life:
Each craven, brave or baffled atom
Offered frank for your inspection
In unconditional surrender
That you accepted with a speechless smile.

Forty minutes, give or take,
We strode that dense seraphic air—

No self, one mind.
                              Then slept and woke
In early evening, light enough
To guess your face and you guess mine—
Familiar grounds, separate as twins.
   I think we called our daily names;
I know we proudly thanked ourselves.
No other mention, then or since,
Of a grace to match man's acquisition
Of the use of fire or the principle
That trees make wood and wood feeds flame
Or Adam's retrospect of Eden
From the stony ground he'd dig for bread.

Ten years gone, four more meetings,
Earnest tries with wiser minds
And grand results in grander rooms
But not again—never, none,
With no one else, not that cellular
Transmigration when willing you
And willing I made of our selves
One sizable brief kind holocaust
To be, in one dim rented room,
A speechless broad tall compound creature:
Fragrant, fertile, unforeseen
And soon extinct—its only future,
The white museum of these black lines,
Whatever selves we bear from here
Through later fates in tranquil hands.

No complaint—endless praise,
Thanks the length of this conscious life:
An afternoon's pure desiring;
Entire union, unrestrained.

YOUR EYES

Eyes, kind eyes, young master there in sunlight—
If you would let me kiss them steadily,
Three hundred thousand kisses steadily
Would still not satisfy,
Not if the waiting harvest of your lips
Stood thick as bursting sheaves of summer grain.

after Catullus

LOST HOMES

1. An Iron Bed in Granville County. A girl age twelve.

The night before, he slept in our room—
Mine and my next-oldest sister's room.
Sister was eighteen, aching for twenty
And deep in love. Her beau, about
As thrilling as dust, had phoned up sick
In the midst of supper; so she cried herself
Unconscious by dark. Once Sister slept,
You could entertain a one-ring circus
At the foot of her bed; and all she'd say
In the morning was "I sure did dream
About music all night."
                              Me though, ever
Since Mam died four years ago—
I took a little string of feverish naps
With a lot of lying there wide awake
In the hot or cold dark, forcing my mind
Not to haul out the mean old pictures
I'd already stored too many of:
                              Mam
Trying to bid farewell to five
Children and a broke-up husband
And still crack jokes as her life seeps through
The hot bedclothes and down and gone. Then
The heart attack Dad underwent last year,
His left hand always colder than his right
When he holds your face and searches your eyes.
He'll always say "Girl, who do you love?"
Then he cups your face and tilts it towards him
To hunt your eyes, whatever you say.
Whoever I mention, he understands
It's always him. Even as late

116

As this last afternoon, he asks again.
   Thank Jesus, I come out and say "Oh you!"
His eyes fill up and, before I can
Say something dumb and untrue like "April
Fool!", he somehow vanishes from the room—
Just leaves, no memory of his back in the door
Or any sound.
                    I'm young enough still
To know the world is more than half magic;
So I stand and think "He's changing now,"
Though I don't think how or into what.

So night—deep night, past three o'clock—
I was bolt awake in the cat-fur dark,
Staving off that grade of awful picture
By naming the principal rivers of Asia,
In order by length with tributaries,
When mine and Sister's door spoke once.
It had these hinges older than Hell; so
If you opened it fast, it said
"Goddamn your soul!" Slow as now,
It just said "*Gawwd*" like old country
Preachers addressing His Honor.
                              Nobody
In our town ever locked doors; the only
Crime was suicide. I thought
It was Aunt Dot that came after Mama died
And all but killed us, on a daily basis,
With excess solicitude—you couldn't belch
Without Dot vowing you had TB
And sewing your shroud. She was also prone
To stark nightmares and joined me once
Or twice a month, having undergone
Some plunge through space or—swear to God—
Being wed in public to a strapping buck,
"Black as boiled tar," that all the family
Kept assuring her was white.
                         So I rolled to the wall

And played hard possum, halfway snoring
While Dot slid in beside me and froze.
Then for once I managed to fool myself—
In three more snores, I was truly asleep
And launched on dreams of my own, mainly good.
In honesty I won't specify, though I can vow
Water would have flowed through it somewhere, **warm.**

In all those years between Mam's death
And my leaving home, I spent a big share
Of every night in boats alone
On thick tan rivers or, faster, bound
With a steamer of friends towards what we hoped
Was *The City Called Fair*—that curious name
For my destination always came to me
When I sailed with friends but never alone.

Whoever was with me that last night,
On the same iron bed Mam bore me in,
I ought to have known—that deep asleep—
It couldn't be Dot. Unused as she was,
Dot slept like a fired cookstove in August.
You had to keep turning, to brown yourself even.
But still in what I dreamed that last
Night, I moved through a chalky winter sky
With afflicted trees; and in my wandering
Mind I shivered hard.
                                        A real
Hand reached in like rescue—cool
But warmer than all my dreams—so
I knew it was bound to be somebody else,
Not Dot or my sister. First I wondered
If I was scared—no. I waited for word—
Not even a breath.
                                        Next I wondered
Where it touched me—it rode so light—
And then I guessed it was on my hip,
Somewhere high on the bone, riding easy.

I was on my left side, turned away;
And since the hand never flinched or moved,
I may have wandered off again.

Anyhow next thing I was somewhere else
That took me awhile to recognize—
I had maybe dreamed myself back in real life:
Me as a young girl, lean as a finger.
I lay the same in this same bed
In the same deep dark; but my body was younger
And leaner still—eight or nine years old,
Turned this same way and with this other body
Flat beside me:
            Dad, to be sure,
The same as now but that much younger
And his left hand laid on my hipbone.
My mind hung on in that child's world,
Hoping to know if this was a picture—
An old snapshot—or life, life moving.
I thought *If it's life, one of us will move*;
The hand though was locked like me in dark
In that old place in my old life
Or dream: I still wonder.
               But this last night
When I was finally awake and present—
Well before light—I'll have to say
I understood my partner was Dad:
Dad live, with all his blood pumped through him,
Was next to me in bed in the night.
   Someway I thought the usable truth,
He's just this lonesome; and then I tried
As hard as I could to talk from my mind—
No words, no breath—and say he was welcome;
To say *Stay here as long as you need,*
Take all you need, I need not to fail you.

Like I said, I was twelve. I knew enough.
To be sure, I couldn't know what'd happen

If that grown a man—and my own father—
Had read my mind and set his hand,
Or whatever part of his strong body,
To work his will and take his need.
    I might be one of those TV women,
Every day of the week now, that stands up moaning
In public sight and blames her people
For her own failure to meet bald life
And stay upright on her scarred two legs—
It can be done: I hope to tell you.
    I might have scalded kids of my own
With my grown famishment and passed my hurt
On down the centuries like war and greed.
I might be Mother Teresa, or better,
Be taking my desperate stand in God's
Teeth to blind my eyes to the four-way
Wreck He lets the human creature make
At home and abroad.
                Home was where
I felt I was that final night, with
My dear dad having chose to be
That close to me, his still-unravished
Wakeful bride, the night before he'd
Take his death. It was so near perfect,
So sweet to know, that again I sailed off
Into calm sleep. And when dawn woke me,
He was recently gone—his place on the sheet
Still hot behind him, the press of his head
In the pillow still damp.
                Home—I know
I spoke it out, the actual word
In that thin light.
             It woke up Sister,
And she said "*Gone?* Gone where on Earth?"
    I let her believe it and said "Search me."

Early that evening they brought Dad home
From the floor of the warehouse where he fell

From the highest loft—pitch-down on his face—
And not one spot of blood, one bruise or
A word. He looked fine as polished wood;
And everybody said his heart had failed,
The second ambush he'd waited for.

   Hard as it sounds, I hope it was ambush.
Like a cornered thing, I watched every face
For a glint of news it was something worse—
Nobody but me even seemed to guess
If he chose to dive.

                I'm more than half-sure—
Most days, even now—that a man that young,
That packed with glee and the hope of more,
Would endow me rich as he did in the dark
With that much tender need and trust
And then plunge out of my sight, my life,
The rest of *his* life and the lovely world's.

Even now towards the end of my time,
I can say I've loved life more than half
And pray for more. I've moved through seven
Houses since, with two kind husbands,
A girl and two boys (each boy thatched
With Dad's coarse hair the color of grain).
But in my mind or in the world,
I've still never called but one place home,
One night, one bed.

             I own it tonight
And—widowed again—I'll rest in it deep
If my own heart, that's stood so much,
Will stand me telling you what I've told.

2. *A Single Bed. A Back Street in Venice. Two young men.*

Fifteen or twenty more dollars a night,
They could enact this solemn start
On the Grand Canal, if just in a garret
With a dim slot-window.
                    Still it's Venice—
A clean room with a locked door,
Two tall windows on a dwarf piazza;
And while they hear no actual water,
No lone cry from a spare gondolier,
The family home in which they've found
This private air is more than half-
Adrift on morning (the morning borne
On a tan Adriatic) and yielding, atom
By limestone atom, to the sleepless gnaw
Of an indolent sea yards away.

  The past two nights they shared the room
With a pair of jokey college friends
Who left for Rome in pre-dawn dark.
Now as a light like primal shine
Endows the room—bruised black chairs,
Muddy tile—with a blinding heat
That soon begins to sound in silence,
A Gabrieli bronze fanfare
Climbs both their minds: muffled, slow
As if this ancient cubicle
Has waited eons for their one visit
And will not let this single chance
Expire untasted, unproclaimed.

  Three yards apart, both hear it plain.
Separate, they hope it strengthens round them;
Hope the wizened crone whose pallet
Creaks beyond their massive door
Will snore on through it, unamazed.
Both wonder *Chance for what and how?*
And neither stirs, though the glory
Builds to a reckless pitch and threatens

To stagger, crumble fast.
                              Then the older
(Just turned twenty-three; a former coward,
Chilled and starving) throws off his sheet
And moves to the younger (a month away
From twenty-one), sits on the narrow
Edge of his cot and, finding clear eyes,
Names the day—"Good Friday. Morning."

The younger nods, oblivious
That what he brings to the awful day—
This opulent light, this city noble
As any built—is a head, a face
Of preposterous majesty: fit to be here,
Fit to bear frank human worship,
Worthy goal. The younger smiles,
Slides left to make a narrow harbor,
Says "Then rest."
                      The older thinks
Good Friday rest, accepts the welcome,
Joins this body splendid as the dark
Cadenza flooding down the slatted
Sun that finds both bodies warmer
Now and half as strong
As its own star-born killing shine.

Thirty-three light years fling on—
Older, younger: each can still
Recall the weight of every beam
From that high window, taste the welcome
Salt of healing shine from God
On His death day in that one cheap
Dissolving room, the secret home
They never leave.

3. *A Cleared Ring in the Blue Ridge Mountains. A boy age twelve, now a middle-aged man.*

This ring was here, way before I found it
When I was twelve. I'd packed me a dry lunch
And left at sunup to climb Table Top, not a hero's
Job. She's gentle-sloped and flat when you get
There but thick all over with cedars and briars—
So I thought, so Hedly told me each time
I claimed one day I'd try her (he's my dad
But, this far gone, I'll say the pure truth:
A vicious bastard stalled in my path).

    I took my damned time in the morning chill and kept
My sweater on well past nine when I had to scrabble
The last fifty yards, perpendicular in full
June sun. Wet as I was and both hands cut,
The minute I brought my last foot up and wavered
On top, I tasted a quick wash of sweetness
That I guessed was partly blood in my throat
But mostly the final recognition by a living
Thing that he's found his place, where he ought to be born
If the chance returns.

                I felt it that strong, even standing
Where it looked like Hedly was right again—mean scrub
And briars. I said to myself "Bring the hand-sickle
Next time and clear you a bed." I thought
I'd spend some nights on top and learn
A few things.

            My body was still hairless as iron;
But shortly below my flat breastbone, I felt
A station warming up—some new broadcaster
That was hell-bent on drowning the air with his news.
From the earliest time my mind recalls,
I'd listened hard, more or less every minute, for some
Slight message I'd last out the meanness
Of parents and kids—I mean real blood, drawn
From my body. I'd also known for two hard years
I needed language lessons *fast*. I knew,

When the thing that rules our bodies struck in mine
And stocked me full of a man's ideas and the skin
To use them, I'd need to be ready to cooperate.

   A thing that strong wouldn't speak the tongues I learned
From Hedly and my scared mother (she spoke through him
Most days anyhow, even when I was hooked
To her, sucking—he made her pass her words through him,
Except when he left; and by then she'd forgot
Her own mind and voice).
               So while I tore through underbrush,
I said out loud I'd get to the midst of Table Top
And lay myself out an actual room
With green walls, a floor, all but a roof. Then
I'd be in serious business to start my hunt
For what I'd need in years to come, if my
Child's body really did reach out and be a man.

   It very near killed me, finding the ring, dead
In the midst of that quarter-mile space—a circle clean
As a washed dinner-plate and damned near as round, just gnawed
At the edge with low dogwoods, half-trying to live.
I said right off *It's somebody else's. Haul-ass
Out.*
       But wanting froze my feet in place,
And I frisked it for signs of who or what. No mark
Of a footstep, no fire ashes, just bare sandy dirt
In an O sixteen feet across at the center.
I'd heard of a place called Devil's Tramping Ground
Where nothing live could last, south of Raleigh.

   But also right away, I knew the Devil had never
Set hoof on this Green Table. On her back here
I was safe from him, his henchmen and the humans he'd won.
Any harm would come from the same direction I'd met
It before—man or beast (I've mentioned Hedly
But not the yellow maddog I cornered too close).

   I was no churchgoer, then or now; but I knew
Full well I hadn't *made* the world. So I bowed in the midst,
Then and there, and thanked Whoever cleared
This home and kept it waiting and brought me here

In the throes of my need. And Who- or Whatever signed
You're welcome by sailing a black cloud past the sun
And throwing me into deep night ten seconds. I chose
To read it as *Welcome* at least.

                           The rest of that day,
I scouted the whole of Table Top, telling
Myself any minute I'd stumble on robbers' counting
Or a boneyard of orphans or—the wildest thing—*safety*:
No sign of humankind, though a world of bones
That had to be beasts, that small and fierce.
    By late afternoon I knew if I meant to get down
By dark, I'd better go. Still I took myself
Back to the ring, and one more time I thanked
The sky—I could see it, clear as I'd ever seen:
The bluest perfect hoop above me, *listening*.

Years to come, till I left for life, I'd make
My secret way to the ring, all times and weathers—
Not a human soul knew, unless you count mine (Hedly
And Mother thought I was "hiking"). I'd spend
As long as two nights running, stretched out asleep
In the absolute midst, more times than most boys
Catch a ball. I was twelve and finally seventeen;
It lasted, stronger by the visit, that long.
    And it taught me the following, secret to now.
If I could keep myself clear of dreams
Till the true midpoint of night and dark, I'd glimpse,
At least one time a year, these huge events—
Confirmable deeds—in the sky above me, dim-lit
Battles of Love and Hate where the brave truth wins,
Though it takes most grievous pain and loss.

                              If I
Could last till the instant of day, I stood the chance
Of seeing—once—the population of the air
We breathe, not motes and germs but the hidden
Traffic of good and evil, the angel freight
Of ruin and grace: splendid to watch.

                                And once

My body fledged out full, if I would show
My skin entirely, stand upright in the midst
At noon on the longest day and let the sun
Alone fire me to strow my seed in a high
Arc out to join the dry Earth, I'd guarantee
The future life of humankind and all
Its brethren, live or dead; the streams that—through
My will—would swarm with food for every mouth,
With endless water for our dry throats and the baking
Land, deep as roots drink.
                                    Swear to God,
I know I pushed that far toward entire knowledge,
The perfect service of man and things, entire
Worth to learn the names that unlatch time
Herself and lead to bliss for all good lives,
All harmless things that do brave duty. I was that
Near wild, that near to killing my whole family,
Teachers, schoolmates and that near *right*.
                                    I'm back
There now as I tell you this—forty-odd years since,
Having come this once to see my mother buried
At last, covered neater than even she hoped
Down back of the house she kept so clean no human
Could grow.
                    The ring is swept and bald as ever. I all
But see the print of my young foot. I kneel to hunt
For any sign my seed has bred the least reward—
Nothing, warm sand that honors my touch.
                                    I've seen,
Of course, how blood-red flowers crowd to the barren
Verge of the ring and flaunt a mystery they retain.
They're new, here anyhow—new to me—and only
When I turn to leave do I risk the thought they've
Waited long to thank my childhood and lure
Me home.

SIX MEMORANDA

1. IMPRECATION

That there in a town like the stuporous skull
Of a matricide—coprophagous grubs—
We denied ourselves three days, two nights,
The solace of common skin on skin,
Attainable ease,
And are punished here in words.

2. BED

Display this photo of an unmade bed
In a faceless thirty-five-dollar motel
To three random strangers. Solicit guesses
At the havoc wreaked on helpless cloth—
Lawnmower salesman thrashed by nightmare,
Silver-wedding couple faced east and west
After one perilous commemorative try,
Father and child paused hopeless here
In flight from what had seemed endless home.

Ask me—*Cooling surface of the bottomless tank*
In which you and I first oared down to anchor
In all that was permeable, mutual skin.

3. YOUR LIES

Your lies
To spare me
Spare only the room
In which you crouch—
Desolate child
At a mother's corpse,
Guarding her cold right
To your sole love.

4. YOUR DEBT

You harp on the enormous debt you owe me—
Repayment could be made on easy terms;
But though you've sapped my hours, sapped whole years,
And though your slightest whim has been command,
Still I must walk before you like a shield:
Absorb, turn, take the thrusts that aim at you;
Be sanctuary for you from yourself,
Stand as faithful bondsman for your crimes,
Shoulder burdens you refuse to bear,
Weep tears you ought to weep, kiss your dry eyes.

after Stefan George

5. MONDAY, JUNE THE SIXTH

Huddled above you Monday, June the sixth,
When I had given what I had to give,
I said the truth—"I love you"—in your ear;
Then felt a shudder grate down from your eyes
And offered quickly "If that makes you worse,
Forgive me please."

                  You turned your face aside.
I said "Where are you?"

                     —"Still right here" you said.
—"*How* are you?"

                  —"Been this happy once before."
So I slid down, extended your left arm
And kissed the two scars parallel as rails
Where you had slashed your veins eight weeks before.

6. FAREWELL WITH PHOTOGRAPHS

Time is mainly pictures,
After a while is only pictures.

Five years, for instance—all but two thousand days—
Will resolve to a few dozen pictures in time:
Of which, if ten give long-range pleasure to their veterans,
Thanks are due.

Thanks then for time—
Deep-cut pictures,
Mainly delight.

WINTER

The images of fall are sought in vain—
Have fallen, rot, are locked in winter cold.
The field is blank; the tree that once stood bold
Is cowed by wind but soothed at night by rain.

As I am soothed who rest now at the close,
Hearing the year's last question to the sky,
Waiting the answer to that rising Why?,
Trusting an answer when spring's coming shows.

after Hölderlin

LATE VISIT

I found the old nurse you envied, Mother.
She naps, for good, in weed and scrub;
And the least I owe is a few last flowers.
   The dead chew bitter cuds of pain;
And when November scours the woods,
They're stunned again by our neglect,
Safe as we are, quilted in down
While icy nightmares plow their sleep—
No partner, no low pillowtalk.

Dark and late by the whistling fire,
What if I see her rocking slow?
What if, this blue December night,
I stumble on her curled by the hearth,
Back from her unending bed
To guard with rheumy steady eyes
The child I was, this broken man?
   What do I tell her selfless face
When cold tears pour from empty lids?

after Baudelaire

AN AFTERLIFE, 1953–1988

Thirty-five years, a gory rake—
My parents scrubbed in laughing prime,
The Kennedys, King, sixty thousand
Baffled sons in Vietnam,
The countless thousand sons they offed,
Mobs of flower-handed girls
Keening for rescue, blazing kids,
A normal stock of routine pillage,
Lunacy, rapture, genocide, famine;
And then my legs unstrung, both frozen,
Me flung down to sit through what
May be of time, need, gift.
  But here, a clear warm day, I come
On a hare-brained backward lunge, trucked up
In a black wheelchair by chuckling friends
To scout my youth and hunt the cabin
Where I passed a slow ten summer weeks
With boys smooth as baby birds—
Mild, still naked-hearted toward
A world they'd barely dreamed was mad.

We've got a key from the owner's son;
And once we pass a final gate
Where hemlocks start, I know each rock,
Each fern primeval.
                    No tears yet
But a blunt amazement humps up hot
In my dry mouth. When we break in
On the heart of the place, it's beating still,
Though derelict for more than a decade.
  The eyeless rake only groomed this hill
Where I worked my twenty-first summer—guide

And shield of a dozen tads, ten to twelve,
In a likable bonded warehouse and playground
For bored sprouts in the dogday swelter:
Summer camp.
              Sequoyah after
The red inventor of Cherokee writing,
Laid up half a mountainside
In the floating Smokies by a fierce-eyed saint
And ramrod dreamer—Walton "Chief" Johnson
Never saw a boy whose timbers he
Couldn't shiver and brace for stiff headwinds:
Manhood! Seize it! God's high hope!
Your very name is on His lips!

Chief's daunted too, buried uphill
In magnanimous block-high hemlocks
Straight as the hope he nursed for man.
The swarms of boys are random-sown
Through a turgid world that may or may not
Be one amp of voltage brighter
For his husky ardor, sleepless labor,
The force of this nursery he gouged by will
From granite and the hearts of trees.
   I've been away since that last morning,
August 1953, when I
Left to lurk for two more years
At home and college; then the headlong
Spiky trail of my getaway, the mottled
Roll of Chased and Caught—trawling
Love in phosphorescent cities,
Unthinkable limbs and music dense
As baled swansdown or sunbaked mire—
Through that much time: no bitter month.

Same eye today, same skull—I hunt
Chief's house, the office, sick bay, lodge,
Library, crafts house, breezy low dining hall,

Oval ballfield, a waving swell
Of foot-deep turf uphill to the cabins
Propped on stilts.
     I try to see
Two hundred yards toward where I guess
My cabin stood. Young blue cedars
Fog the view, but I point that way.
 And my tall friend says "Here you go."
Two more join and, while I cheerfully
Yell "No need," they lug me up.
The chair rolls game on ground rough as gator
Hide.

   It's there. Steps rotted, roof pocked,
Charming as a hatchet-built filagree box
But efficient as watchworks, host to nothing
Bigger than mice, squirrels, the brindle
Panther.
     A friend says "Ready?"
         I think
He means "To roll downhill.' And set
On stemming a risky flood, I say "You
Bet."
    Three bearers lift me, levitate
Three pulpy steps, park me safe
Inside.
    Thick air, cool as evening,
Brown as dusk—there, *here*
I finally am—thirty-five ticking
Years down a ring road.
      The eight
Bunks swim up first from murk—
Four two-tiered six-foot canvas slings
That once stretched taut to sleep light bodies.
All but one are ready to serve
This moment—vacant, clean and dry

(One's torn and fallen, the one that bore
My sole bedwetter, a chunky towhead).
   Mine, the right-top sling by the door,
Suddenly stops my hungry eyes—
The boy I was those seventy nights,
Crusty with love as a cross with blood.
Hurried taps of the pressure valve
Would spare my mind, my mustang body,
Its devastation one more day;
Then through six hundred dreaming hours—
Tads sighing round me—I'd build designs
For my doomed try at knotting myself
In Gordian toils with a lanky blond,
Noble as Neptune, healthy as lye
And bent on yielding me nothing but shame
When what I craved was joint safety.

(*Safety!* The eros-octane in me,
Spilled and lit, would have jacked the crest
Of this hefty outcrop a quarter-mile higher
In chattering dark and crazed the skins
Of all live creatures in a five-mile arc
Like air-thin china in a runaway kiln.)

One friend, a camper years after me,
Says "Where's the plaque with your boys' names?"
   I say "Plaques came well after my time"
And look to a tidy line of boards
Nailed at the eaves. Dim as we are
With me hunched low, I see no words
And turn again to study my bunk—
The night I rolled in after twelve,
Back from a long day-off in Asheville,
And vaulted into my covers to feel
The chill depths lined with chillier rocks.
Both feet clenched, suspecting worse—

A snapping turtle or frosty snake
Mad for heat and a chance at fury,
Fond welcome home from the comatose boys.

A friend says "Ah! The Great Memory falters!"
He's stretching a match to the webby heights—
A brown plaque, maybe nine by five
And older than most, apparently blank.
But then he reads, a blind child groping:
"1953—Reynolds Price, Counselor—
Paul Auston, Jim Avary,
Ed Grimsley, Buddy McKenzie,
Tommy More, Raiford Baxley,
Terry Brookshire, George Harrell,
Jonathan Lindsay, Lester Shepherd.
Ten-week campers: Bill Barrington
And Randy Floyd."

Stunned as a beef at the abattoir door,
I hear the dead names hurtle through me—
Searing, healing, possibly both.
  As six friends gang at the wonder site,
I sink in merciful isolation
And watch a line of figures scramble
From an unsuspected open grave—
A dozen boys, twelve heads for the names,
Big teeth, chopped hair, a team of voices:
None cracked, each laughing, not a tear
In the loaded days.
                    And none from me,
All-Purpose Font, those days or now.
Halfway uphill, jigged in pain,
I'd wondered coldly why I shanghaied
A weekend's rest for a retrograde,
Dead-sure to appall—*Broke-Down Me*
Hunts Me At the Full: hard boy, primed
For a life that looked in this pure air

Plainly unending, a noonday glide,
But ran a quick hot thirty-one years
Toward an unmapped iron murderous wall
That ended me.

Here though, reborn—
Amply friended, spoiled as a pasha,
Unmanned in a fecund afterlife—
I watch the boys' eyes sink again;
And I hear these lean words, mute though clear,
The pitch of Hopkins' "Felix Randal":
How far from then forethought of, all
Thy more boisterous years.
Boisterous, good
To see, starved as a stoat and wild
To couple—for *chance*, bliss, mayhem—
Impeccably kind and cruel as the child
I'd only just been: now this snowcapped
Hulk on wheels.

How far from then
Forethought of. But grand.

Before a friend can turn from the wall
And smile down toward me, I watch the coals
Of my sequestered phoenix pyre
Flare inside me, light for every
Soul in darkness.
Grander still—
Young, I stood here, cocked but blank.
Old, I sit in a hole my green
Self cut in this clean air, seeing now
In my new head a sight my green mind
Never dreamed—the eyes, lips, talons,
Rampant songs and muffled names
Of incontestable angels hid
Past this roof, past the blue abyss—

From all but me, the sole relay
For man on Earth and earthly beasts
Of seraph hymns in adoration,
Praise, undying blame and glee.
I breast their scalding tides of anguish,
Drink their essence—pain and promise,
Grace and torment—
                    Know the back
Of God's right hand (my teeth still taste
His acrid blood), know Death will somedays
Stall at a door if strong eyes bay him;
Know he marks strict time in silence,
Final friend.

                    One live friend moves,
"Sure, let's take it." His broad hand reaches
For the coded plaque still aimed at time,
A plucky voyager.
                    My own hand lifts,
Unspeakably strong, to stop him there.
"It lives here. Leave it." I trust they see
The choice is mine, a power earned
In walking toward the boiling core
On shards of broken mirrors barefoot;
Then returning, charred but me.
Let this pine board endure its earned
Fate in place here—bearing its news
To silence, nestlings, the stone-deaf adder.

My friend's hand drops, though no friend kneels
And no head nods to the solar flare
That fuses light herself with time
Behind my brow, this bony ridge
That bears the fire—outright knowledge
Of how to stay and how to leave,
What to hold and when to loose:
The only secret, *utter loss*;

Glad surrender of every hope but the life
That, breath by slow sweet breath, confounds
An end.

I blink a long instant,
Rig my grinning mask to join them—
Affable gimp.

Two more minutes,
They bear me out and down again,
Heavy but likewise potent as pig iron.
Flung toward dark, a homing bird.

REYNOLDS PRICE

Reynolds Price was born in Macon, North Carolina in 1933. He was reared and educated in his native state, taking his A.B. from Duke University. In 1955 he traveled to Merton College, Oxford where he studied English literature for three years as a Rhodes Scholar. He then returned to Duke and began the teaching which he continues as James B. Duke Professor of English.

In 1962 his novel *A Long and Happy Life* appeared. It received the William Faulkner Award for a notable first novel and has never been out of print. In ensuing years he has published seven more novels, most recently *The Tongues of Angels*. In 1986 his *Kate Vaiden* received the National Book Critics Circle Award. He wrote poems from early adolescence but published his first volume *Vital Provisions* in 1982. His second *The Laws of Ice* appeared in 1986; and his poems have won the Levinson, Blumenthal and Tietjens awards from *Poetry*. He has also published volumes of short stories, plays, essays, translations from the Bible and a memoir *Clear Pictures*. He has written for the screen and television, and his trilogy of plays *New Music* premiered at the Cleveland Play House in 1989.

He is a member of the National Academy and Institute of Arts and Letters. His books have appeared in sixteen languages.